MW01702946

SRA **Specific Skill Series**
for Language Arts

Research

Leveled Books
in Nine Key
Language Arts Skill Areas

SRA
Columbus, OH

The McGraw·Hill Companies

Cover: ©Tim Flach/Getty Images, Inc.

SRAonline.com

McGraw Hill SRA

Send all inquiries to:
SRA/McGraw-Hill
8787 Orion Place
Columbus, OH 43240-4027

Printed in the United States of America.

ISBN 0-07-601718-4

2 3 4 5 6 7 8 9 MAZ 08 07 06 05

TO THE TEACHER

GENERAL INFORMATION ON RESEARCH

The ability to ask questions and use an effective research process to find and present conclusions is a vital skill for students as they progress through school and in later life. In addition to traditional sources, the Internet has provided society with an overload of information. The task of today's student is to find appropriate information and use it to answer questions and solve problems. Knowing how to find, summarize, and present information makes the difference between a good student and a poor student.

Teaching students how to conduct research can be divided into two groups: research skills and research processes. Research skills are related to gathering appropriate information. These include learning to use books and other print materials, charts, graphs, surveys, and the Internet. In the research process, students employ research skills. An effective research process includes getting ideas; asking appropriate questions; narrowing a topic and formulating a research statement; gathering, evaluating, and outlining information; taking notes; summarizing; drafting paragraphs; and writing a bibliography.

ABOUT *SPECIFIC SKILL SERIES FOR LANGUAGE ARTS*

Specific Skill Series for Language Arts is a companion to ***Specific Skill Series,*** a supplemental reading program that has been widely recognized for its effectiveness for over thirty years. The two series are designed and organized the same. ***Specific Skill Series for Language Arts*** consists of discrete units of practice exercises that target and reinforce fundamental language-arts skills. Units in both series are presented in multiple-choice format for standardized test practice.

ABOUT *RESEARCH*

The scope and sequence for Books A through H of *Research* focuses on research skills and processes. The scope and sequence for each book is located on the last page of the book. Each unit includes

- **rule boxes** that explain research skills and processes.
- **models** in each rule box to illustrate the skills and processes.
- **multiple-choice exercises** for skills practice and reinforcement.

Four **Language Activity Pages** (LAPs) appear in each book. Each LAP is divided into the following four sections and reviews the skills practiced in the preceding units:

Exercising Your Skill reviews key terms and concepts.

Expanding Your Skill provides mixed practice.

Exploring Language shows how the skills apply to real-world contexts by featuring one of six forms of writing: descriptive, narrative, personal, persuasive, expository, and poetry.

Expressing Yourself includes two creative activities related to the skills. One activity is always a Work-with-a-Partner activity to encourage collaborative learning.

TO THE TEACHER

SERIES COMPONENTS

- **Student Editions:** Nine books in each level (A–H) focus on nine skill areas: *Grammar, Usage, Mechanics, Spelling, Vocabulary, Sentences, Paragraphs, Writing Process,* and *Research.*
- **Placement Test Books:** One book for each skill area includes diagnostic tests to place students in the correct level.
- **Teacher's Manual:** Primarily an answer key, the *Teacher's Manual* also includes reproducible student worksheets and further information on how to use the program, including classroom management tips.

HOW TO USE *SPECIFIC SKILL SERIES FOR LANGUAGE ARTS*

Placing Students in Levels: The scope and sequence, complexity of skills, and readability in Levels A through H correspond to Grades 1 through 8. Students may, however, be placed in any level. For example, in the second grade, a student who needs remedial work in a specific skill may be placed in Book A, an on-level student who would benefit from skills reinforcement may be placed in Book B, and an advanced student who is ready for enrichment may be placed in Book C or higher. *Placement Tests* help place students in the correct level.

Setting: This series can be used for independent study and one-on-one practice sessions, as well as in small-group and whole-class settings. It is also effective in after-school and summer-school programs.

Getting Started: Students must have notebook paper or copies of reproducible student worksheets (located in the *Teacher's Manual*) before they begin working. Remind students not to write in the books. Students may begin in any unit of any book, depending on the skill practice they need, although it is recommended that they begin with Unit 1. As they work through the units, students should record their answers on notebook paper or on the student worksheets.

Pacing: Students should be encouraged to work at their own pace, completing a few units every day or every other day.

Scoring: Teachers should score units as soon as they have been completed. Then a discussion can be held in which students justify their answer choices.

Internet Use: Some activities, especially those in *Research,* require students to use the Internet. Students' use of the Internet should be monitored closely for content appropriateness and safety.

TO THE STUDENT

Research is asking questions about a topic and then finding the answers. To find the answers, you need to know how to use different sources, including books, magazines, and the Internet. This book will show you how to research a topic.

In Book F *Research,* you will learn about

- Getting Ideas, Narrowing Topics, Formulating Questions, and Making Research Statements
- Finding Information
- Using a Table of Contents
- Finding Newspaper and Magazine Articles
- Key Word Searching
- Evaluating Web Sites
- Reading Graphs and Charts
- Comparing Information across Sources
- Taking Notes and Summarizing
- Writing an Outline
- Writing Paragraphs
- In-Text Citations
- Writing a Bibliography

After you complete this book, you will know how to write an outline to organize the main points of a research report. Part of an outline is shown below.

Clouds

I. Types of Clouds
  A. Cumulus Clouds
    1. found in globular masses; resemble pieces of cauliflower
    2. often extend very high in the sky
    3. associated with fair weather

  B. Cirrus Clouds
    1. wispy; high in the sky
    2. contain tiny crystals of ice; form high in the atmosphere where the temperature is low
    3. may appear shortly before a change in the weather
  C. Nimbus Clouds
    1. rain-bearing; appear dark and dense
    2. term *nimbus* can be added to names of other clouds
  D. Stratus Clouds
    1. flat layers like a blanket
    2. form relatively near Earth's surface
    3. often connected with stormy weather

By mastering the skills in this book, you will know more about using sources of information and planning and writing a research report.

Unit 1

Getting Ideas and Narrowing a Topic

The first step in the research process is to **get an idea.** You might be assigned a research topic, or you might need to come up with one on your own. Ideas for topics can come from almost anywhere—stories or articles you have read things you have always wondered about, activities you enjoy.

- A good research topic is one that requires you to learn something new, evaluate the information you find, and draw your own conclusions instead of just list facts.
- A good research topic is also not too broad, or general. Your topic should be narrow, or specific, enough to write about in one research report, but not so narrow that you will not have enough ideas to write about.

    Broad (General) Topic: Sports
    Narrow (Specific) Topic: The History of Softball
    Topic That Is Too Narrow: How Fast a Softball Can Travel

Answer each question by imagining that you are writing a report about each given topic.

1. Which is *not* the best way to narrow the topic *Transportation* for a report?
   (A) The Railway System: Will It Exist in 100 Years?
   (B) Hybrid Cars and How They Work
   (C) Safe Travel on the Subway
   (D) Ships

2. Which is *not* the best way to narrow the topic *Nutrition* for a report?
   (A) The Nutritional Value of Cereal
   (B) Should People Eat Red Meat?
   (C) Nutrition and Food
   (D) Why Yogurt Is Good for You

3. Which is the best way to narrow the topic *Countries* for a report?
   (A) North American Countries
   (B) Countries around the World
   (C) Small Countries
   (D) Malta, One of the World's Smallest Countries

4. Which is the best way to narrow the topic *Geography* for a report?
   (A) Earth and All Its Features
   (B) Kents Cavern: The Most Important Cave in Northern Europe
   (C) Earth's Lands
   (D) The History of Earth

5. Which is the best way to narrow the topic *Animals* for a report?
   (A) Mammals
   (B) Reptiles
   (C) The Llama, a Fascinating Animal
   (D) Fish

6. Which is *not* the best way to narrow the topic *Scientists* for a report?
   (A) Scientists in the Eighteenth Century
   (B) How Sir Isaac Newton's Discoveries Changed the World
   (C) Theano, the Earliest Female Mathematician
   (D) American Environmentalist Rachel Carson and Her Valuable Work

7. Which is the best way to narrow the topic *Books* for a report?
   (A) The Best Books of All Time
   (B) Fiction and Nonfiction Books
   (C) The Controversy Surrounding Mark Twain's *Huckleberry Finn*
   (D) Books and Libraries

8. Which is *not* the best way to narrow the topic *Famous Singers* for a report?
   (A) The Andrews Sisters: "America's Wartime Sweethearts"
   (B) Famous Jazz Singers
   (C) The Distinctive Voice of Frank Sinatra
   (D) Marian Anderson: The Metropolitan Opera's First African American Soloist

9. Which is the best way to narrow the topic *Medicine* for a report?
   (A) Doctors and Medicines
   (B) Is Ritalin a Safe Medication for Children?
   (C) The Origins of All Medicines
   (D) Every Medicine Ever Made

10. Which is the best way to narrow the topic *Leadership* for a report?
   (A) American Presidents
   (B) Famous People
   (C) Great Leaders
   (D) The Leadership of Benazir Bhutto, Pakistan's First Female Prime Minister

Unit 2
Formulating Questions

After you have narrowed your topic, think about what you want to learn about the topic you chose. Ask questions related to your topic that you want to investigate.

- What might you want to know about the topic *Hawaii?*
  What are important resources in Hawaii?
  Who lives in Hawaii?
  What factors made the United States decide to make Hawaii a state?
- Each question you research should be related to your topic. If your topic is *Hawaii,* you would not ask the question, *What are some other islands in the Pacific Ocean?*

Choose the question that is *not* specifically related to each topic.

1. Dentists
   (A) What do dentists do?
   (B) What other professions have to do with tooth care?
   (C) What classes do students take in college to become dentists?
   (D) When do dentists usually decide they want to be dentists?

2. Rugby
   (A) Are players allowed to carry the rugby ball?
   (B) Why is rugby so popular?
   (C) What are the five most dangerous sports?
   (D) How many players are on a rugby team?

3. Hurricanes
   (A) Where do hurricanes happen?
   (B) What causes a hurricane?
   (C) Are any parts of the world safe from hurricanes?
   (D) How many people does the Coast Guard rescue each year?

4. The Country of France
   (A) What is the culture of France like?
   (B) What does the word *petite* mean in French?
   (C) Does France have a democracy?
   (D) Is France an important ally of the United States?

5. Pottery
   (A) What is the most expensive pottery in the world?
   (B) Why does a potter use a kiln?
   (C) How long does it take to fire a pot?
   (D) What is art?

Unit 2
Formulating Questions

6. The Rain Forest
   (A) What is being done to save the rain forests?
   (B) What kinds of clouds are rain clouds?
   (C) What kinds of plants and animals are found in rain forests?
   (D) On which continents are rain forests located and why?

7. Sailing
   (A) What types of pollution are found in the ocean?
   (B) How does a sailboat work?
   (C) Do you need a special permit to sail on any of the Great Lakes?
   (D) How do you steer a sailboat?

8. Writing
   (A) What are the steps in writing a short story?
   (B) Why is being able to write well an important skill?
   (C) What was the purpose of the first computer?
   (D) How do you choose your topic?

9. Telephones
   (A) Who invented the telephone?
   (B) How different are telephones today from the earliest telephones?
   (C) How has the telephone changed our world?
   (D) What communications technologies have been developed this year?

10. Lewis and Clark, American Explorers
    (A) How long did Lewis and Clark's expedition last?
    (B) What impact did their expedition have on the United States?
    (C) What did Lewis and Clark discover?
    (D) How clean is the Missouri River?

11. Snakes
    (A) Where are snakes found?
    (B) What do snakes eat?
    (C) What are the basics of lawn care?
    (D) How many different kinds of snakes are there?

12. Piano
    (A) How much does a piano cost?
    (B) Is the piano the most difficult instrument to play?
    (C) How many keys are on a piano?
    (D) How hard is it to become the conductor of an orchestra?

Unit 3
Making a Research Statement

Once you have questions about your topic, you can write a **research statement,** or a thesis statement, based on your questions. Then your research can prove or disprove your statement. A thesis is like a hypothesis in science, which you prove or disprove by conducting a scientific experiment.

Research Statement	Question
Martin Luther King Jr. is America's greatest hero.	Who has been America's greatest hero?

Which question is the basis for each research statement?

1. The most populated cities in the United States are near major water sources so people will have water to survive.
   (A) How many people live in Phoenix, Arizona?
   (B) What causes certain American cities to be so large, in terms of population?
   (C) What are the least populated states in the United States?

2. More American citizens live in the southern states than in the northern states because it is easier to live in warm climates.
   (A) How many people live in Florida?
   (B) How cold do the northern states get in the winter?
   (C) Why do more Americans choose to live in the South?

3. There are more large cities in the northern United States than in the southern United States because immigrants settled in the North.
   (A) How has immigration affected the population distribution in the United States?
   (B) What kinds of jobs do most immigrants to the United States get?
   (C) What are the current immigration laws in the United States?

4. The states in the United States with the lowest population are the coldest states.
   (A) How many people live in Alaska?
   (B) What are the populations and the average temperatures of each state in the United States?
   (C) Does weather affect where people live in the United States?

5. California is the most populated state in the United States because it has a good climate and is near the ocean.
   (A) Why do so many people live in California?
   (B) What are the largest cities in California?
   (C) How big is California?

Unit 3
Making a Research Statement

6. Wyoming is the least populated state because it is so cold there.
(A) How many people live in Wyoming compared to the other states?
(B) What is the capital of Wyoming?
(C) What national parks are in Wyoming?

---

7. Since 1850 New York has been the most populated city in the United States because of immigration and industry.
(A) Why do so many people live in New York City?
(B) What kinds of industries have their headquarters in New York?
(C) What is the capital of New York?

---

8. Los Angeles has grown faster than New York because it has a better climate and more area in which to grow.
(A) How did air conditioning affect population growth?
(B) Why is Los Angeles growing faster than New York City?
(C) How many people live in Los Angeles?

---

9. Large cities like Cleveland, Pittsburgh, Detroit, and Buffalo have lost population since 1950 because industry has moved south and overseas.
(A) How many people live in Detroit?
(B) Can cities that used to be large find ways to begin growing again?
(C) What factors have caused people to move away from large cities like Cleveland?

---

10. After air conditioning became widespread, many southern cities started growing.
(A) What caused southern cities to grow in the 1950s and beyond?
(B) What is the average temperature of each of the states in the United States?
(C) What is the average rainfall of each southern state in the United States?

---

11. Some states, such as Pennsylvania, North Dakota, and West Virginia, have stable populations because they have stable jobs and little immigration.
(A) What are the most stable jobs in the United States today?
(B) What are the major cities in Pennsylvania?
(C) Why do some states experience little population growth?

---

12. Arizona and Nevada had the fastest growing populations in the 1990s because people moved there to enjoy a better climate all year long.
(A) What kinds of recreational activities are popular in western states like Arizona and Nevada?
(B) Why have so many people moved to Arizona and Nevada in the last twenty years?
(C) What are the largest cities in Arizona and Nevada?

Unit 4
Finding Information

Once you have a research statement, you need to gather information to prove or disprove your statement. There are many different sources of information in addition to books. Most of the sources listed below can be found on the Internet or at a library.

- An **almanac** includes lists, statistics, facts, and figures. You would use an almanac to find the name of the president of Nicaragua.
- An **atlas** is a book of maps. You would use an atlas to find what lakes are located in France.
- An **encyclopedia** includes general information about many topics. Encyclopedia entries may be one paragraph to several pages long. Encyclopedia entries do *not* include information about current events.
- An **expert** is someone who is especially knowledgeable about a topic. Most experts work in a professional setting. Interviewing an expert is one way of researching a topic for a report.
- A **newspaper** mainly reports on current events. Some newspapers, such as *The Washington Post,* focus on reporting news from around the nation and around the world. Smaller, local newspapers focus on reporting local news.
- A **magazine** includes feature articles on current events or other topics of interest. Feature articles are similar to newspaper articles, but they are usually longer and provide more details.

Choose the best source to use to find each type of information. If both are good sources for that kind of information, choose *Both.*

1. general information about microscopes
   (A) atlas
   (B) encyclopedia
   (C) Both

2. what people's lives were like in England during the Middle Ages
   (A) a history professor (expert)
   (B) almanac
   (C) Both

3. general facts about the Canada Goose and its habitat
   (A) encyclopedia
   (B) atlas
   (C) Both

4. the location of the island of Haiti
   (A) encyclopedia
   (B) atlas
   (C) Both

5. the most common ailments people seek treatment for in your community
   (A) doctor (expert)
   (B) encyclopedia
   (C) Both

6. the population of the largest city in the world
   (A) atlas
   (B) almanac
   (C) Both

7. opinions about a recent decision made by the president of the United States
   (A) magazine
   (B) newspaper
   (C) Both

8. what a leopard eats
   (A) encyclopedia
   (B) zookeeper (expert)
   (C) Both

9. the history of Minnesota
   (A) encyclopedia
   (B) atlas
   (C) Both

10. what was happening in the world on the day you were born
   (A) newspaper
   (B) encyclopedia
   (C) Both

11. what an ecosystem is
   (A) atlas
   (B) encyclopedia
   (C) Both

12. where the rivers in Virginia are located
   (A) atlas
   (B) magazine
   (C) Both

The First LAP

Language Activity Pages

A. Exercising Your Skill

You have been learning how to get ideas for a research report, narrow a topic, formulate questions, develop a research statement, and find information to prove or disprove your research. Number your paper from 1 to 3, and answer the following questions about what you have learned.

1. Which of the following pairs of topics are in order from broad to narrow?
   (A) Government → How a Bill Becomes a Law
   (B) Lady Bird Johnson's Concern for the Environment → Famous Americans
   (C) The History of Golf → Sports

2. What should you do when formulating questions based on a topic?
   (A) Think of only three questions.
   (B) Ask questions you want to know the answers to.
   (C) Include questions that are *not* related to your topic.

3. Which type of source would *not* provide information about current events?
   (A) magazine
   (B) encyclopedia
   (C) newspaper

B. Expanding Your Skill

Number your paper from 1 to 3. Then choose the best source to use to find information on each given topic.

1. when the full moons are this year
   (A) atlas
   (B) almanac
   (C) Both

2. the capital of North Korea
   (A) atlas
   (B) encyclopedia
   (C) Both

3. why whales travel north in the summer
   (A) marine biologist (expert)
   (B) encyclopedia
   (C) Both

C. Exploring Language

Expository Writing Read the following paragraph from a research report. Then answer the questions.

The population in the United States is moving toward warm climates. Since the 1950s when air conditioning became more widespread, large cities in states such as Ohio, Michigan, and Pennsylvania have lost population, while cities in Texas, Arizona, Florida, and California have been growing at a rapid pace. Between the years of 2000 and 2002, for example, Texas's population grew by 4.5%, but Pennsylvania's grew by a mere 0.4%. Only seventeen percent of the land in the United States is part of the warm coastal zone, and about fifty-three percent of the total population lives on this land.

1. What central question does the paragraph answer?
   (A) How many immigrants enter the United States each year?
   (B) How is the population shifting in the United States?
   (C) How many people live in the United States today?

2. What is the best research statement for this research report?
   (A) The population in the United States is shifting from states with varying climates to states with warmer climates.
   (B) Texas and Florida are the fastest growing states.
   (C) People can live in warm climates if their homes are air-conditioned.

3. What is the best source to use to find information for this research report?
   (A) a nonfiction book about Texas
   (B) a magazine article about population trends in the United States
   (C) an atlas that includes a map of the United States

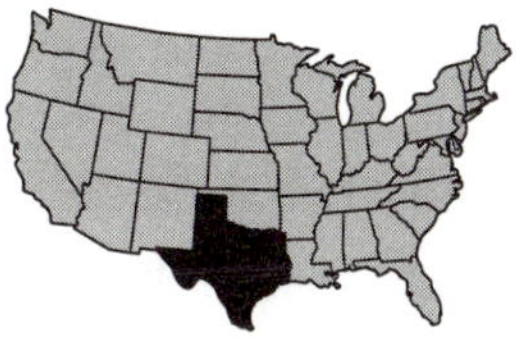

D. Expressing Yourself

Choose one of these activities. When you are finished, give your paper to your teacher.

1. WORK with a PARTNER Work with a partner to brainstorm an idea for a research topic. Then write at least three questions about the topic. Next, write a research statement. Finally, list at least three sources you could use to find information for your topic.

2. Make a list of three topics you would be interested in researching. Formulate three questions you could ask about each topic.

Unit 5
Using a Table of Contents and an Index

To do research, you need to know how to use resources to find information. You can use a **table of contents**, located in the front of a book, to find chapters and their page numbers. An **index**, located in the back of a book, can be used to find the exact page number for a topic. An index is in alphabetical order.

Use the table of contents below to answer the questions.

Air, Weather, and Climate

1. Which chapter provides information about how meteorologists use equipment to determine in advance whether or not a tornado or hurricane will strike?
   (A) Chapter 1 **(C)** Chapter 5
   (B) Chapter 3 **(D)** Chapter 6

2. Which page would you turn to for information about the layers that make up Earth's atmosphere?
   (A) 6 **(C)** 26
   (B) 12 **(D)** 46

3. Which chapter provides information about how meteorologists determine the daily weather forecast?
   (A) Chapter 6 **(C)** Chapter 3
   (B) Chapter 4 **(D)** Chapter 1

4. Which page would you turn to for information about how changes in weather and climate impact different parts of the world?
   (A) 46 **(C)** 72
   (B) 60 **(D)** 6

5. Which chapter provides information about what causes wet and icy weather conditions?
   (A) Chapter 1 **(C)** Chapter 3
   (B) Chapter 2 **(D)** Chapter 4

Unit 5
Using a Table of Contents and an Index

Use the index below to answer the questions.

Index

6. Which page would you turn to for information about weather balloons, which are instruments used to predict the weather?

(A) 12 **(C)** 50
(B) 13 **(D)** 68

7. Which page would you turn to for information about what happened when a specific hurricane reached land?

(A) 72 **(C)** 78
(B) 82 **(D)** 81

8. Which page does *not* provides information about cumulonimbus clouds?

(A) 54 **(C)** 65
(B) 55 **(D)** 80

9. Which page would you turn to for information about cars that are fueled by hydrogen?

(A) 21 **(C)** 23
(B) 22 **(D)** 58

10. Which page does *not* provide information about the weather activity associated with severe storms?

(A) 52 **(C)** 80
(B) 77 **(D)** 83

Unit 6

Finding Newspaper and Magazine Articles

You can use a **periodicals index** to find magazine and newspaper articles about a topic. Many of these indexes are found on the Internet or in a library. A search of the index brings up a list of **citations.** A citation provides information about an article.

A citation often gives the following information: the title of the article, the author of the article, the title of the magazine or newspaper in which the article appears, the volume number of the magazine or newspaper, the issue number of the magazine or newspaper, the page numbers of the article, the date the magazine or newspaper was published

ARTICLE TITLE — AUTHOR — MAGAZINE TITLE — VOLUME NUMBER

Grasslands in the United States. | P. Martinez. | *Geography Magazine* | v10
n6 | p138–143 | Apr. 2004

ISSUE NUMBER — PAGE NUMBERS — DATE

Below is a list of citations from a periodicals index. Use the list to answer the questions

BIRDS

Bird-watching in North Iceland. D. Armstrong. *National Geographic Traveler* v3 n9 p9–13 Sept. 2003

Choosing the Right Bird Seed. Shirushi Cho. *USA Today* v22 no9 p51–53 May 4 2003

How the National Audubon Society Protects Our National Heritage. C. Stewart. *Bird-watching Today* v18 n10 p224–226 Aug. 2002

Migratory Birds Herald Spring. E. Takashi. *Sacramento Bee* v103 n34 p27–28 Mar. 7 2004

New Sibley Guide to Birds Is Extraordinary (Book Review). G. Chin. *Time* v31 n2 p47–49 Apr. 2004

Spotting the Blue-Winged Warbler. I. Anstaett. *Kids and Science* v50 n4 p11 June 2002

1. Which article is the shortest?
   (A) "New Sibley Guide to Birds Is Extraordinary"
   (B) "Bird-watching in North Iceland"
   (C) "Migratory Birds Herald Spring"
   (D) "Spotting the Blue-Winged Warbler"

2. Which article would be a good source of information about the type of seed Cardinals prefer to eat?
   (A) "New Sibley Guide to Birds Is Extraordinary"
   (B) "Bird-watching in North Iceland"
   (C) "Choosing the Right Bird Seed"
   (D) "Migratory Birds Herald Spring"

3. Which article is the most recent?
   (A) "Migratory Birds Herald Spring"
   (B) "New Sibley Guide to Birds Is Extraordinary"
   (C) "Spotting the Blue-Winged Warbler"
   (D) "How the National Audubon Society Protects Our National Heritage"

---

4. Which article is from a newspaper?
   (A) "Bird-watching in North Iceland"
   (B) "Choosing the Right Bird Seed"
   (C) "Migratory Birds Herald Spring"
   (D) "New Sibley Guide to Birds Is Extraordinary"

---

5. In which publication does the article about the National Audubon Society appear?
   (A) *Bird-watching Today*
   (B) *Sacramento Bee*
   (C) *Time*
   (D) *USA Today*

---

6. In which publication was the book review published?
   (A) *Bird-watching Today*
   (B) *Sacramento Bee*
   (C) *Time*
   (D) *National Geographic Traveler*

---

7. Which article would be a good source of information about an exotic location where unique birds can be observed?
   (A) "Bird-watching in North Iceland"
   (B) "Choosing the Right Bird Seed"
   (C) "Migratory Birds Herald Spring"
   (D) "How the National Audubon Society Protects Our National Heritage"

---

8. On what page does the article published in *Time* begin?
   (A) 9
   (B) 27
   (C) 51
   (D) 47

---

9. Which article was written for a younger audience?
   (A) "How the National Audubon Society Protects Our National Heritage"
   (B) "Spotting the Blue-Winged Warbler"
   (C) "Migratory Birds Herald Spring"
   (D) "New Sibley Guide to Birds Is Extraordinary"

Unit 6
Finding Newspaper and Magazine Articles

Below is a list of citations from a periodicals index. Use the list to answer the questions.

CHILDREN

Advances in Health Care for Premature Babies. R. Chavez. *New York Times* v94 n103 p72 June 6 2004

Be Smart about Your Money. L. Owens. *Kids Magazine* v9 n8 p34-37 Aug. 2003

Dinners Kids Love. J. Plant and F. Berg. *Parents* v77 n9 p214-216 Sept. 2002

Don't Spend That Allowance! M. Chase. *By Kids, For Kids* v21 n4 p130-133 Dec. 2004

How Safe Are Our Youngest Athletes? D. Noonan. *Newsweek* v140 n12 p50 Sept. 2002

A Kid's Life: Afghanistan. M. Zackowitz. *National Geographic World* n 317 p26-29 Jan./Feb. 2002

Little League Season Begins. B. Byron. *Sports Illustrated* v16 n83 p14-21 Mar. 2004

Playful Puppets Preschoolers Can Make. *Better Homes and Gardens* v80 n1 p121-122 Jan. 2002

Safety and Your Children. P. Wilson. *Parents* v19 n39 p51-56 Apr. 2004

Safety Play: Know about Your Kid's Sports Program. E. Cooper. *Better Homes and Gardens* v80 n7 p198 July 2002

10. In which month was "Be Smart about Your Money" published?
    (A) January
    (B) March
    (C) April
    (D) August

---

11. Which article is the longest?
    (A) "Don't Spend That Allowance!"
    (B) "Little League Season Begins"
    (C) "Safety and Your Children"
    (D) "Advances in Health Care for Premature Babies"

---

12. Which article would be a good source of information about craft making with two and three-year-olds?
    (A) "Be Smart about Your Money"
    (B) "Playful Puppets Preschoolers Can Make"
    (C) "A Kid's Life: Afghanistan"
    (D) "Don't Spend That Allowance!"

Unit 6
Finding Newspaper and Magazine Articles

13. Which article is from a newspaper?
 (A) "Safety and Your Children"
 (B) "Dinners Kids Love"
 (C) "Advances in Health Care for Premature Babies"
 (D) "Safety Play: Know about Your Kid's Sports Program"

---

14. What is the volume number of the article written by Owens?
 (A) 9
 (B) 16
 (C) 19
 (D) 94

---

15. Which article is co-authored (written by more than one person)?
 (A) "Safety Play: Know about Your Kid's Sports Program"
 (B) "Dinners Kids Love"
 (C) "Playful Puppets Preschoolers Can Make"
 (D) "A Kid's Life: Afghanistan"

---

16. What is the issue number for the article published in July 2002?
 (A) 198
 (B) 39
 (C) 80
 (D) 7

---

17. In which publication does the article about puppets appear?
 (A) *By Kids, For Kids*
 (B) *Parents*
 (C) *Better Homes and Gardens*
 (D) *National Geographic World*

---

18. Who is the author of the article published in *Newsweek?*
 (A) Zackowitz
 (B) Noonan
 (C) Cooper
 (D) Chavez

Unit 7
Key Word Searching

You can find information more easily on the Internet and in library databases if you use specific **key words.**

- If you are looking for information about mako sharks, you should key *mako sharks* in the search box. If you keyed only *sharks,* you would get a list of Web sites about different kinds of sharks, not just mako sharks.
- To make your search even more specific, use quotation marks around the subject you key in the search box. By keying *"desert animals."* you can make sure you *only* get information about *desert animals.* The search engine will search for Web sites that contain *only* the key words in the order in which you keyed them.
- You can also key the word AND between two words or phrases you are searching. If you key *"desert animals"* AND *conservation,* you will get a list of Web sites about what is being done to help protect desert animals.

Choose the best key words to find Web sites containing answers to each question below.

11. What are some famous mountain ranges in Europe?
    (A) famous AND Europe
    (B) famous AND mountains
    (C) famous AND mountain ranges AND Europe

12. What does a harvest mouse look like?
    (A) harvest AND mouse
    (B) harvest AND pictures
    (C) pictures AND mouse

13. What is some information about the life of Martin Luther King Jr.?
    (A) life AND kings
    (B) life AND Martin Luther King Jr.
    (C) kings AND Martin Luther King Jr.

14. How do you build a bookcase?
    (A) build AND furniture
    (B) how AND build
    (C) build AND bookcase

15. How do camels survive the sandstorms in the Middle East?
    (A) camels AND survive
    (B) camels AND desert
    (C) camels AND survive AND sandstorms AND Middle East

Unit 7
Key Word Searching

16. What are the salmon's migration patterns?
(A) "migration patterns"
(B) salmon AND upstream
(C) salmon AND "migration patterns"

17. How did banks operate in the nineteenth century?
(A) banks AND nineteenth century
(B) banks AND operate
(C) checks AND coins

18. How do baboons communicate?
(A) monkey AND communicate
(B) baboon AND communicate
(C) "communicating animals"

19. How does moss take in moisture to reproduce?
(A) bog AND moss
(B) "moisture moss"
(C) moss AND reproduce AND moisture

20. What is the difference between mountain faulting and folding?
(A) mountain AND faulting AND folding
(B) mountain AND faulting
(C) Earth AND folding

21. How did the praying mantis get its name?
(A) "insect names"
(B) "praying mantis" AND name
(C) bugs AND names

22. How are shooting stars able to enter Earth's atmosphere?
(A) shooting AND stars
(B) "Earth's atmosphere"
(C) shooting stars AND entry AND Earth's atmosphere

23. What was the importance of the Gettysburg Address?
(A) "famous speeches"
(B) Abraham Lincoln AND speech
(C) "Gettysburg Address" AND importance

24. What are the main exports of Belgium?
(A) Belgium
(B) Belgium AND "main exports"
(C) main exports

Unit 8
Evaluating Web Sites

Since anyone can create a Web site, it is important to decide whether the information on a site was written by a reliable source. Some questions to ask when evaluating a Web site include the following:

- *Who is the author?* The author of a Web site should be given on the page. The author can be a person or an organization. If the site does not give enough information about the author, you should *not* trust the information given because it might be biased or inaccurate.
- *Why was it written?* Does the site give only factual information, or is the author stating his or her opinion? If a product is being sold on the site, the information presented might be biased because the author wants you to think his or her products are the best.
- *When was it written?* A Web site should have up-to-date information. Even a new site might contain outdated information, so be sure to cross-check your research with another source, such as an encyclopedia or a current magazine article.
- *Does it have the information you need?* A site about bird-watching in North Iceland is not the best site to use if you need general information about bird-watching.

Is each Web site a reliable source?

1. a Web site about your school's policies written by your school's principal this year
   (A) Yes　　**(B)** No

2. a Web site about the Statue of Liberty written by the New York state tourism director
   (A) Yes　　**(B)** No

3. a Web site about the insect world that doesn't have an author
   (A) Yes　　**(B)** No

4. a Web site about the Florida Everglades written by Jake, a first grader
   (A) Yes　　**(B)** No

5. a Web site about the history of Columbus, Ohio, written by the Ohio Historical Society
   (A) Yes　　**(B)** No

6. a Web site about skin care written by a health care company that sells skin care products
   (A) Yes　　**(B)** No

7. a Web site about the geology of the Grand Canyon written by a fifth grader in South Dakota

(A) Yes **(B)** No

8. a Web site showing a map of the airline routes by the Federal Aviation Agency

(A) Yes **(B)** No

9. a Web site about investing in the stock market written by a person who doesn't give his or her name

(A) Yes **(B)** No

10. a Web site about how to prepare a bibliography written by an English teacher

(A) Yes **(B)** No

11. a Web site about the armed services written by the federal government in 1996

(A) Yes **(B)** No

12. a Web site about skiing written by someone who lives in a tropical region where it never snows

(A) Yes **(B)** No

13. a Web site about the toys cats like best written by the president of a company that manufactures cat toys

(A) Yes **(B)** No

14. a Web site about preparing sushi written by a famous Japanese chef

(A) Yes **(B)** No

15. a Web site about how to be an astronaut written by the president of the Neil Armstrong Fan Club

(A) Yes **(B)** No

16. a Web site about new computer technology written in 2000

(A) Yes **(B)** No

17. a Web site about the safest car you can buy written by Cars, Incorporated, a company that claims to sell "the safest car on the road"

(A) Yes **(B)** No

18. a Web site about bird-watching written by someone who has gone bird-watching once

(A) Yes **(B)** No

The Second LAP

Language Activity Pages

A. Exercising Your Skill

You have been learning about using a table of contents and an index, finding newspaper and magazine articles, using key words to find information on the Internet, and evaluating Web sites. Number your paper from 1 to 3. Choose the word or words that correctly complete each sentence.

1. You should look in _____ to find a list of chapters in a book about modern China.
   (A) an index
   (B) a table of contents
   (C) a periodicals index

2. The best place to look for a magazine article about national parks is _____.
   (A) an index
   (B) a table of contents
   (C) a periodicals index

3. To find the address of the Denver Mint, the best place to look would be _____.
   (A) the Denver Mint Web site
   (B) a periodicals index
   (C) a table of contents

B. Expanding Your Skill

Number your paper from 1 to 6. Decide whether or not each Web site is a reliable source.

1. A Web site about diving written by a former Olympic diver
   (A) Yes **(B)** No

2. A Web site about ocean pollution written in 1999
   (A) Yes **(B)** No

3. A Web site about the history of the British monarchs written by an online encyclopedia
   (A) Yes **(B)** No

4. A Web site about the importance of taking vitamins written by a company that manufactures and sells vitamins
   (A) Yes **(B)** No

5. A Web site about the fashion trends written by a fashion expert and updated last month
   (A) Yes **(B)** No

6. A Web site about fossil hunting written by a well-known paleontologist
   (A) Yes **(B)** No

C. Exploring Language

Expository Writing Read the excerpt from a report below. Then number your paper from 1 to 2, and choose the best key words to find Web sites containing answers to each question.

> Although many states have a lot of people, they also have a lot of land, so the states with the greatest population may not have the greatest population density. For example, Rhode Island is forty-third in population with just over one million people, but it is second in population density because it is such a small state.

1. What states have the greatest population density?
   (A) population AND states
   (B) United States AND population density
   (C) Rhode Island AND density
2. What is the population of the states that have the greatest land area?
   (A) "greatest land area"
   (B) states AND population
   (C) population AND states AND land area

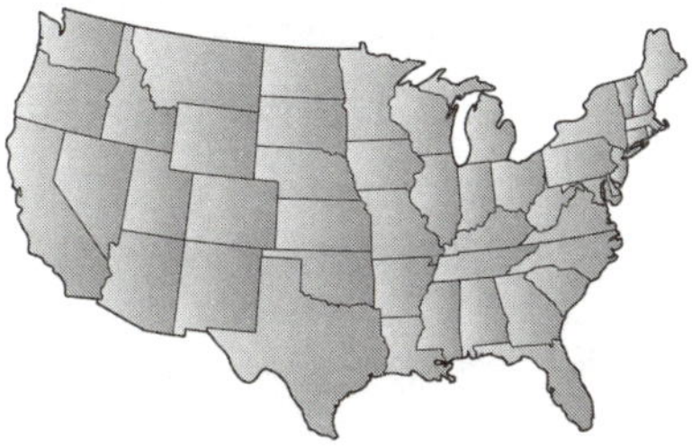

D. Expressing Yourself

Choose one of these activities. When you are finished, give your paper to your teacher.

1. Choose a topic to research. Then use a search engine to find information about your topic. Remember to use specific key words in your search. Make a chart of at least five Web sites related to your topic. List their Web addresses and comments you have about each one.
2. WORK with a PARTNER With a partner, choose a topic to research, such as *pollution.* Then go to the school library to locate a periodicals index, such as the Reader's Guide to Periodical Literature. Look in the index for lists of articles related to your topic. Finally, ask the librarian to help you locate one of the magazine or newspaper articles that was listed under your topic in the periodicals index. Make a photocopy of the article, and write a short paragraph about how easy or difficult it was to use the periodicals index.

Unit 9
Reading Graphs and Charts

Graphs and charts are drawings that give information in a format that is easy to read.

- A **pie chart** shows how a whole can be divided into parts. The main title of the chart is at the top. The specific information this type of chart gives is listed next to or within each segment, or section, of the chart.

Favorite Pizza Toppings

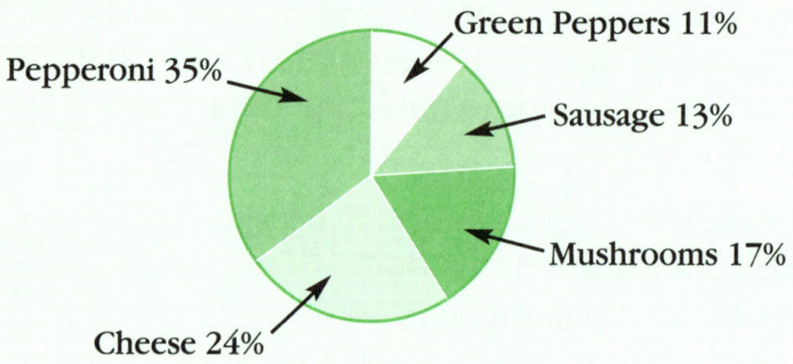

Use the pie chart below to answer each question.

Type of Dogs Shown in the Miyagi Classic Dog Show

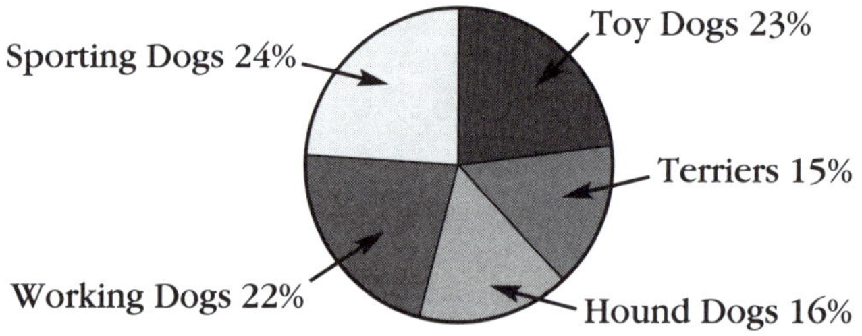

1. Of all the dogs in the Miyagi Classic, which type of dog had the highest percentage of dogs shown?
   (A) Working Dogs
   (B) Sporting Dogs
   (C) Toy Dogs
   (D) Hound Dogs

2. Which two types of dogs combined equal 39% of the dogs shown in the Miyagi Classic?
   (A) Terriers and Toy Dogs
   (B) Sporting Dogs and Hound Dogs
   (C) Sporting Dogs and Terriers
   (D) Hound Dogs and Working Dogs

3. What is the difference in percentage of dogs shown between the Toy Dogs and the Terriers?
   (A) 10%
   (B) 1%
   (C) 9%
   (D) 8%

Unit 9
Reading Graphs and Charts

Use the pie chart below to answer the questions.

Student Participants in Field Day Activities

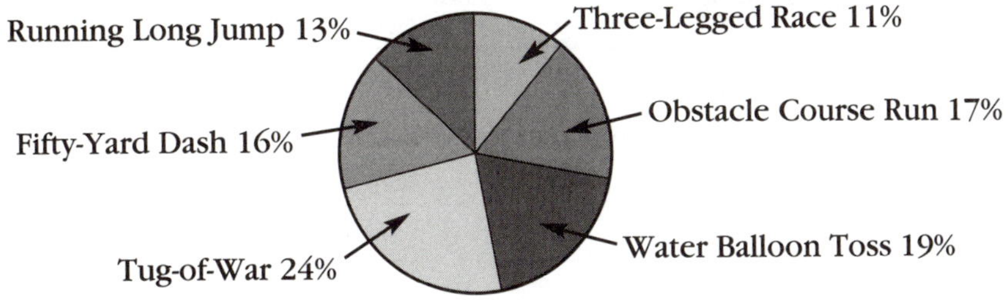

4. What percentage of students participated in the Fifty-Yard Dash?
   (A) 19%
   (B) 16%
   (C) 17%
   (D) 24%

5. Which field day activity was participated in by the largest percentage of students?
   (A) Water Balloon Toss
   (B) Fifty-Yard Dash
   (C) Obstacle Course Run
   (D) Tug-of-War

6. Which two activities were participated in by nearly the same percentage of students?
   (A) Water Balloon Toss and Fifty-Yard Dash
   (B) Obstacle Course Run and Fifty-Yard Dash
   (C) Three-Legged Race and Running Long Jump
   (D) Fifty-Yard Dash and Obstacle Course Run

7. In which two activities *combined* did 24% of the students participate in?
   (A) Obstacle Course Run and Fifty-Yard Dash
   (B) Water Balloon Toss and Obstacle Course Run
   (C) Fifty-Yard Dash and Water Balloon Toss
   (D) Running Long Jump and Three-Legged Race

8. What combined percentage of students participated in the Water Balloon Toss and the Obstacle Course Run?
   (A) 37%
   (B) 36%
   (C) 29%
   (D) 41%

9. Which field day activity was participated in by the smallest percentage of students?
   (A) Water Balloon Toss
   (B) Tug-of-War
   (C) Three-Legged Race
   (D) Running Long Jump

Unit 9

Reading Graphs and Charts

- A **bar graph** uses numbers, lines, and bars to compare information. To use a bar graph, read the title to find out what the graph is about. The information across the bottom of the graph shows the categories that are being compared. The information on the left side of the graph shows amounts.

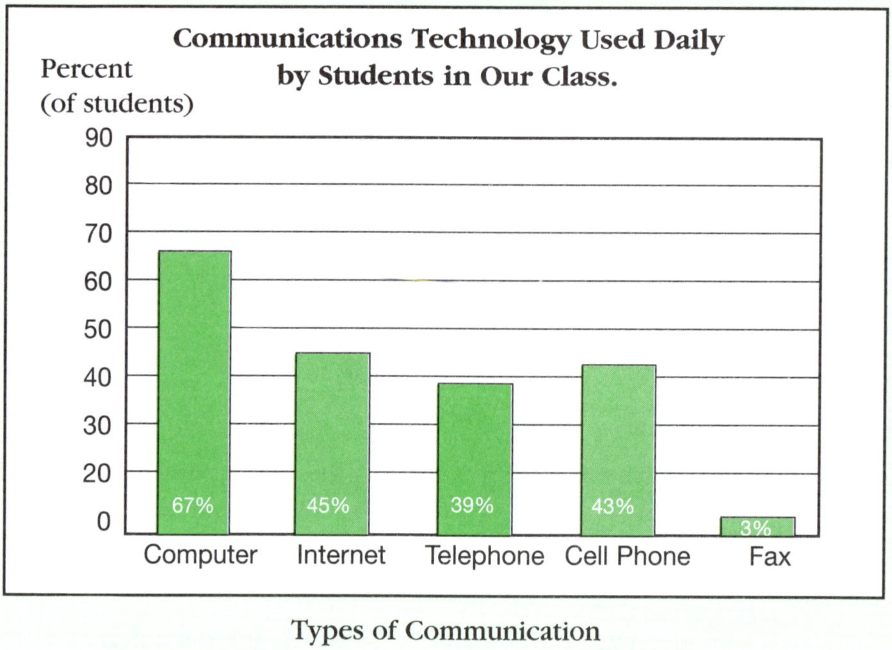

Use the bar graph shown below to answer the questions shown on the next page.

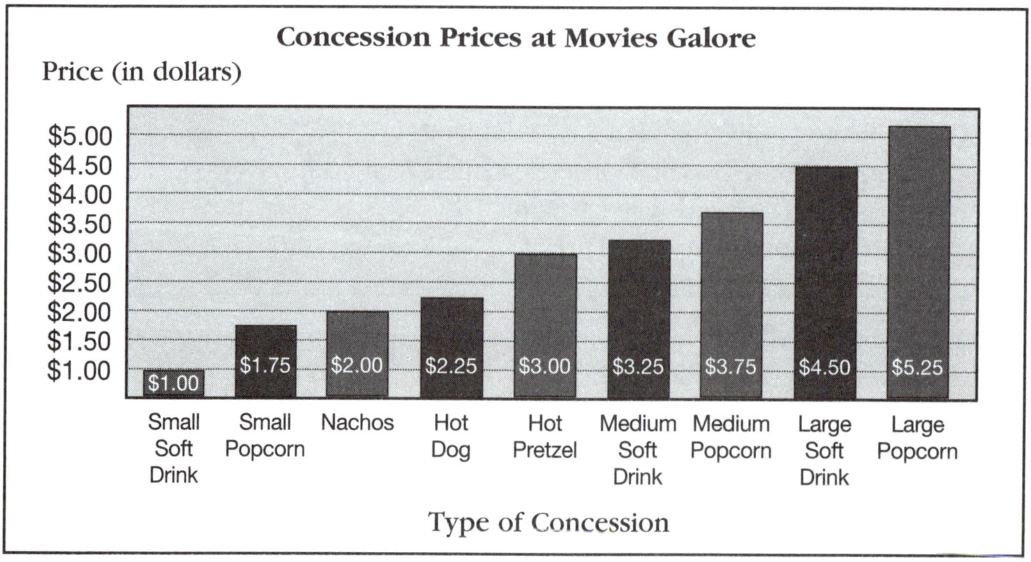

10. For which concession would you pay the most at Movies Galore?
(A) large soft drink
(B) large popcorn
(C) nachos
(D) hot pretzel

11. What is the price difference between a large soft drink and a medium soft drink?
(A) $1.75
(B) $2.00
(C) $1.25
(D) $0.75

12. How much money would you need to bring if you were planning on purchasing a medium soft drink, a small popcorn, and a hot dog?
(A) $9.25
(B) $7.25
(C) $5.00
(D) $8.50

13. For which purchase would you spend the least amount of money?
(A) a small soft drink, a hot pretzel, and a medium popcorn
(B) a large soft drink, a medium popcorn, and a hot dog
(C) a medium soft drink, an order of nachos, and a small popcorn
(D) a hot dog, an order of nachos, and a large soft drink

14. Between which two concessions is the price difference the greatest?
(A) a medium soft drink and a large soft drink
(B) a small popcorn and a hot dog
(C) a large popcorn and large soft drink
(D) a hot dog and a medium soft drink

15. If you brought $5.75 with you to Movies Galore, which concessions could you afford to purchase?
(A) a large soft drink and a hot dog
(B) a medium soft drink and a medium popcorn
(C) a medium popcorn and a hot dog
(D) a medium popcorn and an order of nachos

16. How much more money would you need to bring if you were planning on purchasing a medium popcorn and a medium soft drink instead of an order of nachos and a large soft drink?
(A) $0.25
(B) $0.50
(C) $0.75
(D) $1.25

Unit 10
Comparing Information across Sources

When you are preparing a report, you often must use several sources to find the information you need. Sometimes you need additional sources because you need more information, and sometimes you need to check information from one source by using another source.

Read the following three sources of information about the history of medicine, and then answer the questions.

Time Line

The History of Medicine

Prehistory
Prehistoric peoples think evil spirits cause disease.

Ancient World
Egyptians attempt to provide rational explanations for the causes of disease. The development of writing allows them to record symptoms and cures.

400s B.C.
Hippocrates stresses the importance of observation, diagnosis, and treatment.

1543
Flemish doctor Andreas Vesalius publishes *The Fabric of the Human Body,* the first book to accurately describe human anatomy, including the skeletal, muscular, and nervous systems. He becomes known as the father of anatomy.

1673
Dutch scientist Antonie van Leeuwenhoek builds a microscope that can magnify over 200 times. Leeuwenhoek is credited for discovering bacteria.

1796
English physician Edward Jenner discovers a vaccine to prevent smallpox.

c. 1864
French chemist Louis Pasteur demonstrates that germs cause disease.

1895
German physicist Wilhelm Roentgen discovers X-rays.

1929
Scottish scientist Alexander Fleming develops the antibiotic penicillin.

1953
James Watson and Francis Crick discover DNA.

Unit 10
Comparing Information across Sources

Web Site

The History of Medicine

Historical evidence can tell us about some of the diseases that afflicted prehistoric peoples, but little is known about how illness was thought of or treated. What is known is that people believed that evil spirits were responsible for causing disease. Because there was no writing system, symptoms and cures of disease were not recorded, and it was difficult to pass on knowledge. Much later, the Egyptians attempted to give reasons for the causes of disease, even though they still attributed many illnesses to spiritual rather than physical causes.

By about 400 B.C., as Greek civilization developed and reading and writing became more widespread, distinguished scientists and writers began to be identified. Hippocrates was one of these persons. He began a new approach to medicine by insisting that medicine be seen as a science rather than a religion and by eliminating the gods as a cause of illness and disease. He stressed the importance of observation, diagnosis, and treatment. Hippocrates also believed in getting fresh air, a healthful diet, and exercise to build strong, healthy bodies.

The scientific method was developed in the sixteenth century. This process emphasized looking for explanations through observation and experimentation. One of the first persons to use the scientific method was Andreas Vesalius, a professor of anatomy. He based his drawings of the human body on his own dissections of humans, not animals as had been done in the past.

The invention of the microscope in the seventeenth century brought about many discoveries. Doctors and scientists could observe tiny living organisms not previously seen. Roentgen's discovery of the X-ray in 1895 let doctors view inside the body without having to perform surgery.

Probably the greatest discovery is that of the effect of germs in causing disease and vaccines in curing those diseases. Edward Jenner was the first person to introduce cowpox into the bloodstream in order to catch the much more serious smallpox disease. Louis Pasteur developed vaccines for several diseases after he demonstrated for the first time in history that germs cause disease.

The discovery of penicillin by Alexander Fleming in 1928 was one of the major events in the history of medicine. It saved thousands of lives in World War II.

The middle of the twentieth century brought the discovery of DNA, the building blocks of all living things. Scientists can now study single genes. They can test for genetic disorders and treat them. This discovery is thought by many to have the capability of changing the future of medical research.

Encyclopedia Entry

Fleming, Alexander. Alexander Fleming (1881–1955) was born in Scotland, moved to London at age thirteen, and later trained as a doctor. He worked with Sir Almroth Wright, who had discovered an antityphoid vaccine in 1896 and had started an inoculation department at St. Mary's Hospital. Both men went to France during World War I to treat wounded soldiers and could see for themselves that there was no effective way to treat many infections.

After the war, Fleming served as professor of bacteriology at St. Mary's Hospital. He was determined to find a better way of killing germs. In 1928, he was studying staphylococci (bacteria that causes wounds to become poisonous). By chance, he noticed that a mold that had developed on a dish of the staphylococci germs caused the germs to die.

He grew more of the mold, which was later developed into the antibiotic *Penicillium notatum.* Fleming then tested this on animals, with no negative effects, and also used it to cure a colleague's eye infection.

Fleming had discovered the first antibiotic. However, it was not until the research work of Howard Florey and Ernst Chain that penicillin was produced as a drug. At first, supplies of penicillin were limited, but by World War II it was being mass-produced by the American drug industry. By 1944 there was enough penicillin to give all soldiers before active service and for all the allied troops wounded in the D-Day invasion of Europe.

Penicillin is widely used in the treatment of many diseases, including anthrax, meningitis, diphtheria, and pneumonia.

Alexander Fleming, along with Florey and Chain, received the Nobel Prize in Medicine in 1945.

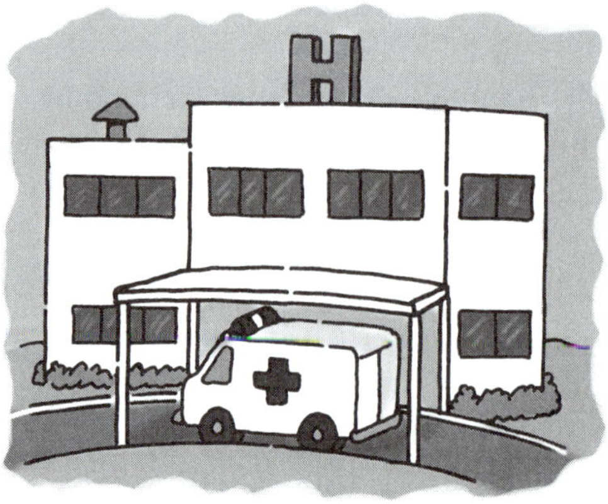

Unit 10

Comparing Information across Sources

1. Which source gives the most information about what Hippocrates taught?
   (A) time line
   (B) Web site
   (C) encyclopedia

2. What is the name of Vesalius's anatomical text?
   (A) *How to Dissect Humans*
   (B) *The Scientific Method*
   (C) *The Fabric of the Human Body*

3. Which source gives the most information about how Fleming discovered penicillin?
   (A) encyclopedia
   (B) Web site
   (C) time line

4. Which source gives the most information about the medical diagnoses and treatment of prehistoric peoples?
   (A) time line
   (B) encyclopedia
   (C) Web site

5. Which source does *not* tell anything about penicillin use in World War II?
   (A) time line
   (B) encyclopedia
   (C) Web site

6. Which sources do *not* tell about the contributions of Florey and Chain?
   (A) Web site and encyclopedia
   (B) Web site and time line
   (C) encyclopedia and time line

7. Which source tells the most about the uses of penicillin?
   (A) encyclopedia
   (B) time line
   (C) Web site

8. What source tells about the importance of the discovery of DNA?
   (A) time line
   (B) encyclopedia
   (C) Web site

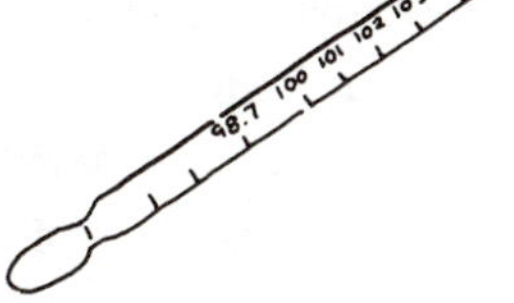

Unit 11
Taking Notes

When you are researching your topic, **take notes** on what you hear or read. Taking notes will help you organize information for a research report. Each note you write should answer a question about the topic of your report.

What are the seven continents?	
—North America	**—South America**
—Europe	**—Asia**
—Africa	**—Australia**
—Antarctica	

Read the following paragraphs. Then complete each note card.

Japan

Japan is a chain of about 4000 islands that form an arc approximately 1500 miles long. China lies east of Japan. To the west, across the Sea of Japan, are South Korea and North Korea. North of Japan are Russian islands. But these neighbors are at a minimum 180 miles from the coast of Japan. Thus, Japan has a long history of geographical and cultural isolation.

Japan has an interesting geography. It has many rivers, most of them short and swift-flowing. Flooding is often a problem, caused by spring snow melting and summer rainfall. Japan also experiences the destructive power of earthquakes, volcanoes, tidal waves, and hurricanes.

The fear of serious earthquakes has led to many changes in building construction. Concrete buildings are replacing wooden buildings that are vulnerable to the quakes' firestorms. Tall buildings must conform to strict standards. Japanese citizens participate in frequent earthquake drills. Families keep fire extinguishers and survival kits ready.

Farming is important in Japan. But because of its small size and its great number of people, farmers use every inch of it carefully. In some places, three crops a year are planted. Farmers terrace their fields and use machinery, fertilizers, and irrigation to enhance the output of their crops. Rice is grown throughout most of Japan, both for consumption and export. Livestock is also an important export. Japanese farmers also produce vegetables, wheat, fruit, and tea.

In the 1960s, Japan developed into a producer of high-technology, high-quality goods and has since captured a large share of the world market. These goods include computers, audio and video equipment, and cameras. In addition, motor vehicles, machinery, and chemicals are some of the country's leading products. Japan is also one of the world's major shipbuilding nations.

Unit 11
Taking Notes

What kinds of natural occurrences affect Japan?	
—volcanoes	—tidal waves
—hurricanes	—earthquakes
—______	

1. Which note completes the note card?
   (A) floods
   (B) avalanches
   (C) drought
   (D) sandstorms

What are Japan's neighbors?	
—North Korea	—Russia
—China	—______

2. Which note completes the note card?
   (A) Thailand
   (B) South Korea
   (C) Vietnam
   (D) India

How do Japanese farmers try to increase crop yield?	
—using fertilizers	—farming on terraces
—irrigating their crops	
—______	

3. Which note goes in the blank on the note card?
   (A) letting fields lie fallow
   (B) rotating crops
   (C) using machinery
   (D) overplanting

How do many Japanese make their living?	
—farming	—building ships
—developing high-tech equipment	
—______	

4. Which note goes in the blank on the note card?
   (A) producing automobiles
   (B) acting on Broadway
   (C) conducting tours of volcanoes
   (D) working on cruise ships

Unit 11
Taking Notes

Read the following paragraphs. Then complete each note card.

Horses

Horses were probably first tamed on the steppes of central Asia between 3000 and 4000 B.C. These first domesticated horses were kept for meat and milk.

As early man began to move around, horses started to be used as pack animals. They then served—and still serve today in many countries—as farm animals. Another major historical use of horses is carrying soldiers into battle. As the use of the wheel developed, horses pulled the two-wheeled chariots with spoked wheels depicted in many movies.

Horses and zebras belong to the equid family, a group that also includes donkeys and mules. Equids are mammals that have long legs, hoofed feet, a flowing tail, and a mane on the upper part of the neck.

Equids have sharp front teeth, which help them feed on grasses. Horses have good eyesight and hearing and a keen sense of smell. They can run at a high speed.

Horses have several names, depending on their age and gender. A young male horse is called a colt, an adult male horse a stallion. A young female is called a filly, while an adult female is a mare.

One popular and beautiful horse is the Appaloosa, noted for its spots and splashes of color. Appaloosas are found in almost every part of the horse world. They set speed records on the race track and excel at jumping, reining, and roping, yet they are gentle family horses, especially good for children.

Native Americans learned to use horses and especially loved the Appaloosa for its intelligence and speed. These horses helped the Nez Perce elude the U.S. Cavalry for several months in the Nez Perce War of the late 1800s. They fled more than 1,300 miles over rugged terrain. When they were defeated, their surviving horses were surrendered to soldiers, left behind, or given to settlers. The number of Appaloosas decreased until a club was formed that now promotes spending time with this wonderful horse.

Another horse that has thrilled crowds at horse shows is the American Walking Pony. It has a rich golden color and a long flowing mane. Its unique gaits include the Pleasure Walk, the Merry Walk, and the Canter. It trots and jumps beautifully as well.

Over the centuries, horses have worked for us and given us much fun and pleasure. We will always appreciate our horses.

Unit 11
Taking Notes

For what have people historically used horses?	
—going into battle	—milk
—meat	—carrying equipment
—______	

5. Which note completes the note card?
   (A) farming
   (B) herding
   (C) mining
   (D) babysitting

What are the attractive points of an Appaloosa?	
—fast	—spots and splashes of color
—good at jumping	—good at reining
—good at roping	—______

6. Which note completes the note card?
   (A) broncing champions
   (B) beautiful solid brown color
   (C) gentle with children
   (D) communicate with their eyes

What happened to the Appaloosa after the Nez Perce were defeated?
—were surrendered to the U.S. Cavalry
—were left behind
—______

7. Which note completes the note card?
   (A) were shipped to Europe
   (B) were given to a club
   (C) were sent to zoos
   (D) were given to settlers

What are the physical characteristics of an equid?	
—long legs	—a mane
—hoofed feet	
—______	

8. Which note completes the note card?
   (A) a flowing tail
   (B) colorful coat
   (C) smooth hair
   (D) walks on two legs

Unit 12
Summarizing

A **summary** briefly reviews the main points of a reading selection. Writers use summaries of information to support their research statements.

- To write a summary, look for the most important points in the selection. Then write them in your own words. Writing about someone else's ideas in your own words is called paraphrasing.

Original Writing

Dolphins are mammals that often swim in the ocean with tuna. Fishing fleets search for dolphins with helicopters and speedboats, hoping to locate schools of yellowfin tuna. When they find dolphins, the fishermen throw out their nets expecting to catch tuna. But they not only catch tuna, they also catch dolphins. Since dolphins are air-breathing animals, they drown when trapped underwater in these nets. In the 1980s, the fishing industry killed 100,000 dolphins a year. Most U.S. tuna boats have stopped using methods that kill dolphins, but some continue to use the nets.

Summary

Because dolphins swim with tuna, they are frequently caught in fishing nets and drown because they are air-breathing animals. Although most U.S. tuna boats have changed their methods to protect dolphins in recent years, some still use nets.

Choose the best summary for each paragraph or group of paragraphs.

1. People use echoes to measure distances in the ocean. A sonar (Sound Navigation and Ranging) device sends out sound waves from ships and measures the time it takes for the waves to bounce off an object and return. Treasure hunters use sonar to locate sunken shipwrecks. The sound waves used in sonar are called ultrasonic. Ultrasonic sounds, or ultrasound, have frequencies that are too high for the human ear to hear.

   Some animals have their own sonar. Bats make ultrasonic noises and use their big ears to catch the echoing sound waves. The echoes help the bat catch food from the air and avoid objects while flying in the darkness. Dolphins use echoes to find or avoid objects in the ocean. They are so good at translating echoes that they can tell the difference between a nickel and a dime dropped into the water.

   (A) Sonar sends out ultrasonic sound waves. The high frequencies of these sound waves are too high for humans to hear.

   (B) Both people and animals use sonar. People use sonar devices at sea to measure distances or to find what remains of a shipwreck. Animals, such as bats and dolphins, use their own sonar to find food or avoid bumping into objects.

   (C) Sonar is used by people and animals.

Unit 12
Summarizing

2. Ocean animals have characteristics that allow them to survive. Ocean animals have also adapted to the high level of salt in their environment. For example, saltwater fish drink a lot of water because they lose body fluids through their skin and gills. They need and use all the water they drink. Freshwater fish are different. They absorb, or take in, water through their skin and gills. Therefore, freshwater fish don't need to drink any water. Some fish, like salmon, smelts, and butterfly mudskippers, can adapt to live in fresh water or in salt water. However, very few fish can make this adjustment.

(A) Animals in the ocean have ways of surviving. They adapt to their environments.

(B) Freshwater fish absorb water, so they do not need to take in water. Some fish can adjust to either environment.

(C) Different kinds of fish must adapt to different environments. Saltwater fish must drink water because of the high salinity in ocean water, but freshwater fish do not need to take in water. Only a few fish can adapt to any environment.

---

3. Arteries are the blood vessels that carry blood from the heart. Veins are the vessels that bring blood back to the heart. As the blood vessels move into the tissues in our body, they get smaller and smaller until only one blood cell can move through the vessel at a time. These small vessels are called capillaries. All of the body's pickups and deliveries happen in the capillaries.

(A) Some blood cells can move through a vessel only one at a time.

(B) Arteries and veins carry blood back and forth to the heart.

(C) The three types of blood vessels are arteries, veins, and capillaries.

---

4. A satellite, such as the Hubble Telescope, is an object that orbits, or revolves, around a larger body in space. There are two types of satellites—natural ones, like the moon, and artificial ones, such as *Sputnik 1*.

To put a satellite into orbit, the rocket carrying it has to go fast enough to carry the satellite high above Earth. The rocket has to go fast because it is fighting the force of Earth's gravity. Gravity is the force that pulls objects toward one another, no matter how small or far apart they are. The force of Earth's gravity keeps you, the moon, and artificial satellites on or circling the Earth. When the satellite reaches a certain point in space, it enters a path or orbit around Earth.

(A) Both natural and artificial satellites orbit the Earth. Artificial satellites must be carried into space by rockets at a high rate of speed to counteract gravity.

(B) *Sputnik I* is a type of artificial satellite. There are also natural satellites, like the moon.

(C) Without gravity, people would not be able to live on Earth, and satellites would not be able to orbit Earth.

Unit 13
Writing an Outline

When writing a report or research paper, it is helpful to write an **outline.** An outline provides a loose guideline for the report. To make an outline, group your information into similar topics. Use each group as a main topic in your outline. Within groups, cluster note cards into subgroups that include details. The subgroups will become subtopics on your outline. Then write details under each subtopic.

- Use capital Roman numerals (*I, II, III, IV,* and so on) for the main topics on your outline.
- Use capital letters (*A, B, C,* and so on) for subtopics, and use Arabic numbers (*1, 2, 3,* and so on) for details. Use lowercase letters (*a, b, c,* and so on) for the second level of details, if you have any.

Use the outline below to answer the questions on the following page.

<u>Planets in the Solar System</u>

I. Mercury
  A. Size and Atmosphere
    1. **J**
    2. no atmosphere because so close to sun
  B. Surface and Other Characteristics
    1. **K**
    2. a desert in which nothing can live

II. Venus
  A. **L**
    1. 12,104 km in diameter
    2. thick atmosphere traps sun's heat making Venus the hottest planet
  B. Surface and Other Characteristics
    1. flat, waterless surface
    2. sometimes called "the evening star" because of its brightness

III. **M**
  A. Size and Atmosphere
    1. 12,756 km in diameter
    2. atmosphere contains nitrogen, oxygen, and water vapor
  B. Surface and Other Characteristics
    1. **N**
    2. oceans and winds help keep temperature moderate

IV. Mars
  A. Size and Atmosphere
    1. 6,787 km in diameter
    2. **O**
  B. Surface and Other Characteristics
    1. red surface because covered with iron-rich rocks
    2. **P**

Unit 13
Writing an Outline

1. Which of these belongs in the space marked **J**?
   (A) ancient Greeks called it Apollo and Hermes
   (B) Mercury was the Roman god of commerce
   (C) second smallest planet—4,878 km in diameter
   (D) surface features cliffs and valleys

2. Which of these belongs in the space marked **K**?
   (A) rocky, cratered surface
   (B) Venus has some mountains higher than Mount Everest
   (C) astronomers are scientists who study space
   (D) scientists not sure how solar system began

3. Which of these belongs in the space marked **L**?
   (A) Earth
   (B) Surface
   (C) Size and Atmosphere
   (D) Color

4. Which of these belongs in the space marked **M**?
   (A) Planets
   (B) Earth
   (C) Distance from the Sun
   (D) Origin of Name

5. Which of these belongs in the space marked **N**?
   (A) atmosphere traps moderate amount of sun's heat
   (B) nine planets total
   (C) atmosphere protects humans from sun's dangerous rays
   (D) only planet with liquid water

6. Which of these belongs in the space marked **O**?
   (A) Ray Bradbury wrote *The Martian Chronicles*
   (B) atmosphere contains mostly carbon dioxide and nitrogen
   (C) there may have been life on Mars
   (D) space aliens

7. Which of these belongs in the space marked **P**?
   (A) deep canyons mean that liquid water was once there (not there now)
   (B) exploration rovers *Spirit* and *Opportunity* arrived there in 2003
   (C) Mars was Roman god of war and agriculture
   (D) inspired H.G. *Wells's The War of the Worlds*

Unit 13
Writing an Outline

The following outline continues the outline from page 42. Use this outline to answer the questions on the following page.

V. Jupiter
  A. Size and Atmosphere
    1. largest planet—142,800 km in diameter
    2. **Q**
    3. atmosphere has layers of liquid hydrogen
  B. Surface and Other Characteristics
    1. large red spot that is a permanent storm on surface
    2. **R**

VI. Saturn
  A. Size and Atmosphere
    1. 120,660 km in diameter
    2. atmosphere mostly hydrogen and helium
  B. **S**
    1. **T**
    2. lightest planet; less dense than water and could float

VII. Uranus
  A. Size and Atmosphere
    1. 51,000 km in diameter
    2. atmosphere mostly hydrogen, helium, and methane
  B. Surface and Other Characteristics
    1. **U**
    2. tilted on its axis more than any other planet

VIII. Neptune
  A. Size and Atmosphere
    1. 49,500 km in diameter
    2. atmosphere similar to Uranus
  B. Surface and Other Characteristics
    1. faint greenish-blue color in sky
    2. **W**

IX. Pluto
  A. Size and Atmosphere
    1. **X**
    2. thin atmosphere of methane
  B. Surface and Other Characteristics
    1. similar in appearance to Triton, Neptune's largest moon
    2. rocky core surrounded by water-ice and methane-ice

8. Which of these belongs in the space marked **Q**?
   (A) Greek god Zeus is identified with Roman god Jupiter
   (B) rings discovered by Voyager I in 1979
   (C) Galileo Galilei discovered four of Jupiter's moons
   (D) eleven times larger than Earth

9. Which of these belongs in the space marked **R**?
   (A) asteroids orbit the sun, mostly between Mars and Jupiter
   (B) thick clouds, lightning, swirling winds
   (C) Earth and Mars have seasons
   (D) Zeus is a weather god

10. Which of these belongs in the space marked **S**?
    (A) Rings
    (B) Moons
    (C) Surface and Other Characteristics
    (D) Meteoroids, Asteroids, and Comets

11. Which of these belongs in the space marked **T**?
    (A) atmosphere like Earth's atmosphere long ago
    (B) second largest planet
    (C) acronyms can help you remember names of nine planets
    (D) spectacular, wide rings made of icy particles

12. Which of these belongs in the space marked **U**?
    (A) names means "sky"
    (B) surface looks green due to fog
    (C) about the same size as Neptune
    (D) fog in atmosphere caused by gases

13. Which of these belongs in the space marked **W**?
    (A) has Great Dark Spot that is large rotating storm
    (B) fourth largest planet
    (C) Neptune was Roman god of the seas
    (D) Neptune's largest moon, Triton, has ice volcanoes

14. Which of these belongs in the space marked **X**?
    (A) astronomers predicted its existence before they found it in 1930
    (B) closest approach to sun will occur in the year 2236
    (C) smallest planet—2,253 km in diameter
    (D) very little known about Pluto

The Third LAP
Language Activity Pages

A. Exercising Your Skill

You have been learning about reading pie charts and bar graphs, comparing information across different sources, taking notes, summarizing, and writing an outline. Number your paper from 1 to 4, and answer the following questions about what you have learned.

1. What is *not* an advantage of comparing information across different sources?
   (A) Sources may have different points of view.
   (B) Some sources may have more information than others.
   (C) One source may not be fun to read.

2. What is *not* an advantage of taking good notes from sources of information?
   (A) You need the exact words of each source.
   (B) Notes help you remember where you read certain information.
   (C) Notes help build an outline that supports your research statement.

3. What is the main advantage of outlining a research paper before you write?
   (A) An outline organizes your information and arguments.
   (B) An outline can be used as a table of contents.
   (C) An outline uses Roman numerals.

4. What is the advantage of summarizing information?
   (A) A summary focuses on the main ideas of a body of information.
   (B) A summary can be used as an outline.
   (C) A summary does not have to be written in your own words.

B. Expanding Your Skill

Choose the best beginning for an outline that is organized well and supports the research statement below.

1. Cincinnati, Ohio, is a great place to live.

   (A) I. People and Places
   A. Places to Visit
   1. Eden Park
   2. Union Terminal
   3. Cincinnati Art Museum

   (B) I. People and Places
   A. Geography
   1. weather
   2. once called the Queen City
   3. has a professional baseball team

C. Exploring Language

Expository Writing Read the paragraph below. Then choose the best summary for the paragraph.

New Jersey is called the Garden State for a good reason. Not only does it have very fertile soil that produces tomatoes, blueberries, peaches, and peppers, it also has over two million acres of beautiful forest. Even though New Jersey is a small state, it has a diverse landscape. The Appalachian Valley and the Palisades offer a mountain experience, and the 127 miles of Atlantic Ocean beaches provide year-round recreation. Many different people choose to live in New Jersey because it is such an interesting state. Some of the most famous Americans have roots in New Jersey, including Thomas Edison, Paul Robeson, Walt Whitman, Frank Sinatra, and Bruce Springsteen. New Jersey is a great place to live or to visit.

(A) New Jersey has 127 miles of beaches along the Atlantic coast. Walt Whitman is one famous American who had his roots in New Jersey.

(B) New Jersey is a small state, but it is beautiful. People should visit it.

(C) The features that make New Jersey a great state to live in or visit include its beautiful, fertile landscape, its mountains, and its beaches. It has been home to many famous Americans.

D. Expressing Yourself

Choose one of these activities. When you are finished, give your paper to your teacher.

1. Think of three questions to ask about a state or a country. Use a search engine to find Web sites that answer your questions. Then look up your topic in an encyclopedia. Compare the information you found on the Internet and in the encyclopedia. Tell your class about what you found.

2. WORK with a PARTNER Find information about a state or a country in five different sources. Evaluate and compare the different types of information you found. Present your findings to the class.

Unit 14

Writing Introductory Paragraphs

Once you have done your research and written an outline of your ideas to prove or disprove your research statement, you are ready to start writing. As you write, you may find you need to do more research to support your case.

- A simple way to organize your research paper is in five paragraphs. The **introductory paragraph** includes your research, or thesis, statement. The next three paragraphs are **supporting paragraphs** and present your arguments. The **concluding paragraph** summarizes your arguments and restates your research statement.
- The introductory paragraph is important because it explains what your research is about and why it matters. A good way to organize an introductory paragraph is like a funnel.

Broad statement that tells the importance of your topic
The arguments against your topic
Research or thesis statement

Choose the best thesis statement for each introductory paragraph.

1. In 1900 only 4.1% of the population was over sixty-five. In 2000 12.4% of the population was over sixty-five. United States Census projections are that by 2010 the percentage of people over 65 will be 13.2% and by 2050, the percentage will be 20.3%, the largest of any age group. Some people think that society should direct the majority of its efforts toward supporting younger people because they represent the future.

   (A) The United States Census makes population projections, and by 2050 there will be more people over sixty-five than any other age group.

   (B) Although much attention is focused on youth culture and young adults, attention must be paid to providing services and care for the growing percentage of people over sixty-five.

   (C) The percentage of people over sixty-five is growing because people are having fewer babies.

2. In 1960, 35% of women and 52% of men aged eighteen to twenty-four lived with their parents. In 2000, 47% of women and 57% of men of the same age group lived with their parents. Although some may think that today there are stronger family ties, this situation is caused by the cost of living.

   (A) More men than women aged eighteen to twenty-four live with their parents.

   (B) At an increasing rate, young adults cannot afford to live on their own.

   (C) Family ties are stronger today than they were forty years ago.

3. In 2000, 10% of all households consisted of five or more people, down from 21% in 1970. Many people think this is due to more affordable housing. This situation, however, is related to birth rates.

(A) People are having fewer children than they were in 1970.

(B) The number of people per household dropped over 10% in thirty years.

(C) There are fewer people per household today than in 1970.

---

4. In 1970, 46% of households had only one or two people. In 2000, that number rose to 59%. Some may think this is because people want their own space, but it may have to do with the number of births.

(A) The percentage of couples who choose not to have children has grown dramatically over the past thirty years.

(B) There are more one or two person households today than there used to be.

(C) Today people can afford to live alone.

---

5. According to the official 2000 census, California is the most populated state with thirty-three million people. The least populated is Wyoming with just under 493,000 people. Some may think more people live in California because of job opportunities. Climate, however, is the major reason.

(A) More people live in California than Wyoming.

(B) The weather and climate in California are so pleasant that people want to live there.

(C) Many people choose not to live in Wyoming.

---

6. In 1790, the official census counted 3.9 million people in the United States. In 2000, there were 281 million. This high rate of population growth is largely due to immigration. Immigrants come to America for many reasons, not least of which are its democratic government and the freedoms and opportunities such a government affords. Surprisingly, living in a democracy is not the main reason people immigrate.

(A) Research has shown that the geography and natural resources of the United States are actually stronger attractions to immigrants.

(B) If the number of immigrants from Spanish-speaking countries continues to rise, Spanish may become another official language in the United States.

(C) The United States population has grown by about 277 million over the past 200 years.

Unit 15

Writing Supporting Paragraphs

Once you have written your introductory paragraph and stated your thesis, the next paragraphs in your research paper should support your thesis. You should try to have at least three supporting paragraphs.

- Each **supporting paragraph** should have a topic sentence and evidence that supports the topic sentence. Try to have at least three pieces of evidence to support each topic sentence. Your evidence will come from the research you have done. As you write, you may find you need to do more research to find more evidence to support your statements. The statements that include evidence are underlined in the supporting paragraph below.

Shark products are not needed for human survival. Shark meat is high in protein, but there are many other ways to get protein, such as eggs, milk, and legumes. Other nonessential shark products include shark-tooth jewelry and some lubricants and cosmetics that contain shark liver. We can do without these products. If we did, the demand for shark products would stop.

Choose the best supporting statement for each topic sentence.

1. Throughout history, snakes have struck fear in the hearts of many people.
   (A) The majority of venomous snakes in the United States come from the pit viper family.
   (B) This fear has led to a large number of superstitions and religious myths.
   (C) If you are bitten by a snake, the first thing you should do is wash the bite with soap and water.

2. Some insects are venomous, but their bites or stings are rarely fatal.
   (A) Bee, hornet, and wasp stings hurt but do not cause death unless the victim has a severe allergic reaction.
   (B) Ant bites can hurt a lot.
   (C) If you get stung by a bee, first try to remove the stinger, and use ice to reduce the swelling.

3. Australia has some of the deadliest snakes.
   (A) People rarely die of copperhead or rattlesnake bites.
   (B) Australia's tiger snake and taipan snake bites are almost 100% fatal without antivenom.
   (C) Most king cobra bites don't have enough venom to be fatal.

4. Tarantulas have an undeserved terrible reputation.
   (A) The American tarantula is actually harmless to humans, although its bite can cause some pain and swelling.
   (B) Tarantulas are large hairy spiders found all around the world.
   (C) Some people keep tarantulas as pets.

5. Portuguese man-of-war bites cause severe pain but are not directly fatal.
   - **(A)** The Portuguese man-of-war is a jellyfish-like animal that lives in warm water areas.
   - **(B)** The Portuguese man-of-war has tentacles up to seventy feet long.
   - **(C)** Portuguese man-of-war bites can cause shock that can cause death in rare cases.

---

6. Some people are morbidly afraid of common spiders because they are afraid of spider bites.
   - **(A)** A funnelweb spider is also called a grass spider because it is found mainly in temperate grassland areas.
   - **(B)** What they do not realize is that although funnelweb, black widow, and brown recluse spiders are venomous, most spider bites are harmless.
   - **(C)** Scorpions are different from spiders.

---

7. Many people think Gila monsters are deadly.
   - **(A)** Gila monster bites cause pain and low blood pressure, but people do not usually die from them.
   - **(B)** Gila monsters can be as large as two feet long with a heavy body and tail.
   - **(C)** Gila monsters are found in the southwest United States.

---

8. Several sea animals are venomous.
   - **(A)** Lizards do not live in the sea.
   - **(B)** Varieties of octopus and stingray are venomous but seldom fatal.
   - **(C)** Some snakes live in water.

---

9. Black widow spiders are known for their venom.
   - **(A)** Black widows are small, round-bodied spiders with red hourglass markings.
   - **(B)** Black widows are found in tropical and temperate zones.
   - **(C)** Their venom is extremely poisonous, but it rarely kills humans.

---

10. Cottonmouth water moccasins are found in the United States.
    - **(A)** Cottonmouth water moccasins can grow to five feet long.
    - **(B)** A bite from a cottonmouth snake causes severe pain and swelling but is seldom fatal.
    - **(C)** Cottonmouth snakes live in wetlands of the southern United States from Virginia to Texas.

Unit 16
In-Text Citations

When writing a research report, you must name the sources of the information you are presenting. An **in-text citation** appears within your report and gives information about your sources. Use an in-text citation to cite someone else's exact words or ideas.

- To write an in-text citation, write in parentheses the **author's last name** and the **page number or numbers** on which the information appears in the original source. Each citation should immediately follow the material to which it refers.

  Only some cats enjoy eating catnip **(Froelich 32)**.
- For **two authors**, insert both authors' last names and the page number: (Browning and Froelich 70).
- If there is **no author** credited, use a short version of the title and give the page number: (*Just the Facts* 248).

Use the citations in the report below to answer the questions that follow.

How to Mix a Batch of Potting Soil

Many gardeners, when they decide to pot a plant or two, simply pick up a trowel and mix a small quantity of whatever they need at the moment. They may also choose to buy a sack of ready-to-use mix at the nursery (Grether 45). However, if you do a large amount of gardening or if you are creating some raised beds, "a little shovel-and-wheelbarrow work is needed" (Kimball and Hahn 116). Good potting soil should contain sufficient nutrients for plant growth and development. It should be easy to work and easy for roots to penetrate, and it should be sufficiently porous for water to be absorbed thoroughly yet not so open that water runs through it too rapidly (*Britannica* 1013).

A popular basic mixture consists of two parts good garden loam, one part sand, and one part peat moss (Alexander 43). Certain plants—azaleas and camellias, for example—will not do their best unless the mix consists of at least fifty percent organic matter, such as finely ground bark, peat moss, or leaf mold.

When you are ready to pot your plant, the mix should be damp but not wet. A good test for dampness is the same as the standard one for soil texture: squeeze a handful hard. If it falls apart quickly when the hand is opened, it is too dry. If any water comes out, it is too wet. If it retains its shape as squeezed and simply cracks slightly, it is damp enough (*Basic Gardening* 83).

Unit 16
In-Text Citations

1. Which author or authors talk about using a shovel and a wheelbarrow?
   (A) Alexander
   (B) Kimball and Hahn
   (C) *Basic Gardening*

2. What information does Alexander give?
   (A) where to buy ready-to-use potting soil
   (B) the test for potting-soil dampness
   (C) a basic potting-soil mixture

3. On what page is the *Britannica* information found?
   (A) 1013
   (B) 83
   (C) 116

4. Which author or authors talk about making sure the potting mix is damp but not wet before potting the plant?
   (A) Grether
   (B) *Basic Gardening*
   (C) none

5. What information does *Britannica* give?
   (A) criteria for good potting soil
   (B) how to grow camellias
   (C) the test for potting-soil dampness

6. On what page is the Grether information found?
   (A) 43
   (B) 45
   (C) 83

7. Which author or authors describe how to know if the mix is too dry?
   (A) *Basic Gardening*
   (B) *Britannica*
   (C) none

8. Which author or authors give options for mixing your own soil?
   (A) Kimball and Hahn
   (B) Alexander
   (C) Grether

Unit 16
In-Text Citations

Use the citations found in the report below to answer the questions that follow.

Parties

Parties are most fun when they are built around a clever idea or theme, when everyone participates (Dodson 14), and when informality and friendliness are "the order of the day" (Liston 25). Such parties require careful planning. The larger the group, the more careful the preparation must be (Wilson and Rader 48). Knowing your group—family, friends, work associations—is your "first job" (*Great Parties* 7). Do they like costume parties? Are they an athletic group? Is it someone's birthday or graduation? Is it a retirement celebration? Do they know one another (Smith 36)?

A fun "kid" party for older students or adults is the Mother Goose party. Guests come dressed as Little Bo Peep, Little Boy Blue, Humpty Dumpty, Mother Hubbard, Mary and her little lamb, and other Mother Goose characters. A good mixer game is the Circle of Rhymes game. Start by making two circles, males on the inner circle, females on the outer circle. The two circles move in opposite directions to music. When the music is periodically stopped, the circles face one another, and each person recites the nursery rhyme he or she represents (Harbin 70). Small teams can act out Mother Goose rhymes. Ahead of time, prepare a list of rhymes, and write them on slips of paper. Have the groups choose one. The groups can win prizes based on costuming and creativity in acting out their rhymes (Berry 131). One refreshment idea for the Mother Goose party is "Jack Horner" plum pie. With a little thought, you can plan a fun and memorable party.

9. Which author or authors talk about winning prizes at the Mother Goose party?
   (A) Great Parties
   (B) Wilson and Rader
   (C) Berry

---

10. What information does Harbin give?
   (A) eating "Jack Horner" plum pie
   (B) how to play the Circle of Rhymes game
   (C) what your first job is when throwing a theme party

---

11. On what page is the Wilson and Rader information found?
   (A) 48
   (B) 36
   (C) 131

Unit 16

In-Text Citations

12. What information does Dodson give?
    (A) how parties are most fun when they are friendly and informal
    (B) how parties are most fun when everyone participates
    (C) how important careful preparation is

13. On what page is the Smith information found?
    (A) 70
    (B) 7
    (C) 36

14. Which author or authors talk about things you should know about your guests?
    (A) Smith
    (B) Harbin
    (C) none

15. Which author or authors talk about the importance of preparing carefully for a larger group?
    (A) *Great Parties*
    (B) Wilson and Rader
    (C) Dodson

16. What information does Berry give?
    (A) the name of a good mixer game
    (B) information about winning prizes in a game
    (C) how to make plum pie

17. Which author or authors talk about what you should do first when throwing a theme party?
    (A) Harbin
    (B) Wilson and Rader
    (C) *Great Parties*

18. Which author or authors talk about how to make invitations to a memorable party?
    (A) none
    (B) Wilson and Rader
    (C) Dodson

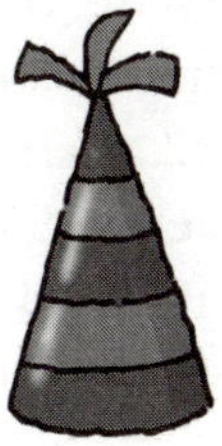

Unit 17
Writing Concluding Paragraphs

A **concluding paragraph** summarizes your research and restates your thesis. The concluding paragraph should explain how you proved your thesis and why it is important.

- A good organization for a concluding paragraph is an inverted funnel.

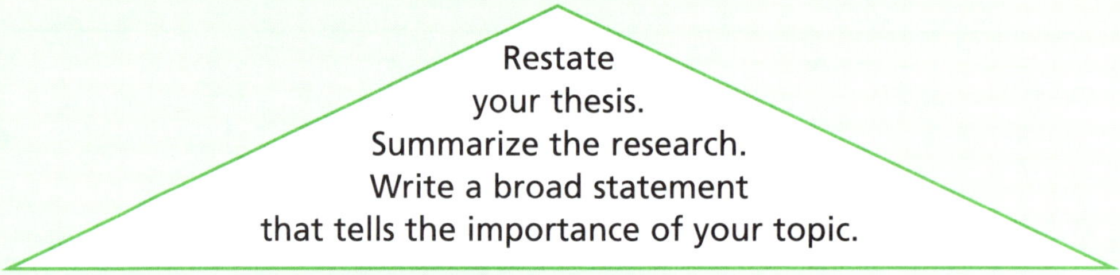

- The following paragraph is organized based on the inverted funnel above.

Although many people think all immigrants should be treated the same, different people require different services. In 1920 the largest number of immigrants to the United States came from Germany. In 1960 the largest number came from Italy. In 2000 the largest number came from Mexico. Immigrants from different cultures have different needs to help them join American society.

Choose the best concluding paragraph for each underlined thesis statement.

1. **(A)** Wind is a potential energy source. The average wind speed at Mt. Washington, New Hampshire, was recorded at 231 miles per hour. Many states average between seven and twelve miles per hour. Harnessing the power of the wind can be the key to renewable energy for the future.
   (B) Wind is a potential energy source. Jacksonville, Florida, averages 7.9 miles per hour. Casper, Wyoming averages 12.8 miles per hour. Chicago, Illinois, which is often called the "Windy City," averages 10.4 miles per hour. Louisville, Kentucky, averages 8.3 miles per hour.

2. **(A)** Lightning is a dangerous weather phenomenon. Lightning kills an average of seventy-three people per year, tornadoes an average of sixty-eight, and hurricanes an average of sixteen. Schools in areas where tornadoes are common have tornado drills in the spring.
   (B) Lightning is a dangerous weather phenomenon. It kills an average of seventy-three people per year. That is more than tornadoes and hurricanes, but because lightning is so common and lightning strikes are rare, people do not guard against them. Even indoors, people should stay away from windows and avoid contact with electricity to protect themselves against lightning, a deadly force.

3. **(A)** Florida has the most coastline of any state outside of Alaska. It has 770 miles of Gulf Coast and 580 miles of Atlantic Coast. California has 840 miles of Pacific Coast, and Alaska has 5,580 miles of Pacific Coast.
(B) Florida has the most coastline of any state outside of Alaska. With over 1,420 miles of coastline, Florida has the advantage of lots of recreational beaches but also the problem of hurricanes and flooding. With its coasts on both sides of the state, Florida must devote special resources for maintaining its coastline.

---

4. **(A)** The birthrate is dropping in the United States. In 1960 the rate was 23.7 births per 1000 people. By 2000, the rate was 14.5 births. Many factors may contribute to this, including people living longer and more people deciding not to have children. People are working hard to project where the trends may be going in the future.
(B) The birth rate is dropping in the United States. It has gone from 23.7 to 14.5 births per 1,000 people in forty years. In 1970 the rate was 18.4, in 1980 the rate was 15.9, and in 1990 the rate was 16.7.

---

5. **(A)** Eating habits have changed dramatically over the past one hundred years. In 1909, twenty-seven gallons of whole milk and seven gallons of skim milk per 1000 people were consumed. In 1999, only eight gallons of whole milk and 13.9 gallons of skim milk were consumed per 1000 people. In 1909, only eleven pounds of poultry per 1000 people were eaten. In 1999, sixty-eight pounds per 1000 people were eaten.
(B) Eating habits have changed dramatically over the past one hundred years. People are drinking skim milk, which contains a lot less fat than whole milk, and they are eating more poultry. These trends may affect not only life expectancy but quality of life as well.

---

6. **(A)** You can get a lot of exercise just doing normal activities. Washing a car for forty-five minutes can give you the same workout that thirty minutes of bicycling, fifteen minutes of jumping rope, or twenty minutes of swimming laps gives you.
(B) You can get a lot of exercise just doing normal activities. Even less vigorous activities, like washing windows, can give you the same amount of exercise as more vigorous activities for shorter periods of time. To maintain physical fitness, just stay active, and that doesn't mean everyone has to run a marathon.

Unit 18
Writing a Bibliography

A **bibliography** is a list of sources used in a research report or other piece of writing. It is usually placed at the end of the piece of writing. Each **citation**, or entry, in the bibliography identifies the name, author, title, publisher, date published, and sometimes the page numbers of the source.

- A bibliography is arranged in alphabetical order by author. If there is no author, alphabetize by title.
- If there are two authors, the first author's name is reversed (last name, first name), but the second author's name is not reversed.
- All lines in a citation except the first one should be indented.

Use the sample bibliography entries to answer the questions that follow.

BOOK

Author's last name, author's first name. *Title of Book*. City and state of publication: name of publisher, year of publication.

Shaffer, Monika. *Washington, D.C.* New York, NY: Travel Press, 2003.

MAGAZINE

Author's last name, author's first name. "Title of Article." *Title of Magazine*. volume number, issue number, date of publication, page numbers.

Rader, Russel and Adam Ward. "Snowboarding." *Life Today*. v. 20, n. 8, Mar.12, 2003, p. 24.

NEWSPAPER

Author's last name, author's first name. "Title of Article." *Title of Newspaper*. volume number, issue number, date of publication, page numbers.

Domingo, Lucia. "Italian Opera Stars at Gala Event." *Philadelphia Gazette*. v. 5, n. 64, Nov. 30, 2003, p.D10.

Unit 18
Writing a Bibliography

ENCYCLOPEDIA

Author's last name, author's first name. "Title of Entry." *Title of Encyclopedia*. Edition or version. If no author given, begin with "Title of Entry."
"Elephants." *World Encyclopedia*. 2005 ed.

WEB SITE

Author's last name, author's first name. "Title of Page." Sponsor. Date written or last update. Date accessed. <Electronic address>.
Orcutt, Carissa. "Real Stars in Sports." *Teen Sports*. April 25, 2004. Accessed June 25, 2004. <http://www.teensportssite.org/realstars.htm>.

1. On what page of the magazine can "Snowboarding" be found?
   (A) 8
   (B) 20
   (C) 24
   (D) D10

2. What is the name of the publication in which the article "Italian Opera Stars at Gala Event" can be found?
   (A) *World Encyclopedia*
   (B) *Philadelphia Gazette*
   (C) *Teen Sports*
   (D) *Life Today*

3. What is the name of the organization that sponsored the Web site about sports stars?
   (A) *Teen Sports*
   (B) *Philadelphia Gazette*
   (C) *Carissa Orcutt*
   (D) *Sports Magazine*

4. On what date was the Web site written?
   (A) March 12, 2003
   (B) November 30, 2003
   (C) June 25, 2004
   (D) April 25, 2004

5. Which citation includes two authors?
   (A) book
   (B) magazine
   (C) newspaper
   (D) Web site

Unit 18
Writing a Bibliography

Answer the following questions about writing a bibliography.

6. Which is the correct way to write a citation for a book?
   (A) Connie Brown. *Westward*. New York, NY: Big Sky, Inc., 2004.
   (B) *Westward.* Brown, Connie. New York, NY: Big Sky, Inc., 2004.
   (C) Brown, Connie. *Westward*. Big Sky, Inc.: New York, NY, 2004.
   (D) Brown, Connie. *Westward*. New York, NY: Big Sky, Inc., 2004.

---

7. Which is the correct way to write a citation for a Web site?
   (A) Munoz, Arnoldo. “Brave Americans.” *American History*. March 22, 2003. Accessed April 30, 2004. <http://www.amerhistory.com/west>.
   (B) Munoz, Arnoldo. “Brave Americans.” <http://www.amerhistory.com/west>. March 22, 2003.
   (C) “Brave Americans.” Arnoldo Munoz. *American History*. March 22, 2003. <http://www.amerhistory.com/west>.
   (D) Arnoldo Munoz. “Brave Americans.” March 22, 2003. *American History*. <http://www.amerhistory.com/west>. Accessed April 30, 2004.

---

8. Which is the correct way to write a citation for a magazine article?
   (A) Adams, Kevin. “The Cattle Drive.” *American Geographic*. v. 17, n. 4, Jan. 15, 2003, pp. 11–13.
   (B) Adams, Kevin. *American Geographic*. “The Cattle Drive.” v. 17, n. 4, Jan. 15, 2003, pp. 11–13.
   (C) Adams, Kevin. “The Cattle Drive.” *American Geographic*. n. 4, v. 17, Jan. 15, 2003, pp. 11–13.
   (D) Adams, Kevin. “The Cattle Drive.” *American Geographic*. v. 17, n. 4, pp. 11–13, Jan. 15, 2003.

---

9. Which is the correct way to write a citation for a book?
   (A) Penny Wilson. *Nat Love*. New York, NY: Blue Books, 2003.
   (B) Wilson, Penny. *Nat Love*. New York, NY: Blue Books, 2003.
   (C) Wilson, Penny. *Nat Love*. Blue Books: New York, NY, 2003.
   (D) *Nat Love*. Wilson, Penny. New York, NY: Blue Books, 2003.

---

10. Which is the correct way to write a citation for a newspaper article?
   (A) Pam Jolley and Patty Smith. “Women Conquer the West.” *Arizona Republic*. v. 82, n. 12, Dec. 13, 2000, p. C4.
   (B) Jolley, Pam and Patty Smith. “Women Conquer the West.” *Arizona Republic*. Dec.13, 2000, p. C4, n. 12, v. 82.
   (C) Jolley, Pam and Smith, Patty. “Women Conquer the West.” *Arizona Republic*. v. 82, n. 12, Dec.13, 2000, p. C4.
   (D) Jolley, Pam and Patty Smith. “Women Conquer the West.” *Arizona Republic*. v. 82, n. 12, Dec.13, 2000, p. C4.

Unit 18
Writing a Bibliography

11. Which is the correct way to write a citation for a Web site?

(A) Michelle Song. "New York to San Francisco." May 22, 2002. University of Pennsylvania. August 9, 2004. <www.ilovehistory.net/research/song.htm>.

(B) "New York to San Francisco." Song, Michelle.University of Pennsylvania. Accessed August 9, 2004. May 22, 2002. <www.ilovehistory.net/research/song.htm>.

(C) Song, Michelle. "New York to San Francisco." May 22, 2002. University of Pennsylvania. Accessed August 9, 2004. <www.ilovehistory.net/research/song.htm>.

(D) Song, Michelle. "New York to San Francisco." University of Pennsylvania. May 22, 2002. Accessed August 9, 2004. <http://www.ilovehistory.net/research/song.htm>.

---

12. Which is the correct way to write a citation for a newspaper article?

(A) Browning, Robert. *New Mexico Daily* "Traveling West." v. 82, n. 12, Dec. 13, 2000, p. F2.

(B) Browning, Robert. "Traveling West." *New Mexico Daily*. v. 82, n. 12, Dec.13, 2000, p. F2.

(C) "Traveling West" by Robert Browning. *New Mexico Daily*. Dec.13, 2000, p. F2, n. 12, v. 82.

(D) Robert Browning. "Traveling West" *New Mexico Daily*. v. 82, n. 12, Dec.13, 2000, p. F2.

---

13. Which is the correct way to write a citation for an encyclopedia?

(A) *World Encyclopedia*. 2005 ed. "Edison, Thomas A."

(B) "Edison, Thomas A." *World Encyclopedia*. 2005 ed.

(C) "Edison, Thomas A." 2005 ed. *World Encyclopedia*.

(D) 2005 ed. *World Encyclopedia*. "Edison, Thomas A."

---

14. Which is the correct way to write a citation for a book?

(A) Brad Hunkler. *Singing Don Quixote*. Detroit, MI: School Press, 1990.

(B) Hunkler, Brad. *Singing Don Quixote*. School Press: Detroit, MI, 1990.

(C) *Singing Don Quixote*. Hunkler, Brad. Detroit, MI: School Press, 1990.

(D) Hunkler, Brad. *Singing Don Quixote*. Detroit, MI: School Press, 1990.

---

15. Which is the correct way to write a citation for a magazine article?

(A) Gabrielle Morales. *Los Alamitos Dispatch*. "Best Toys for Babies" v. 27, n. 1, Nov. 17, 2003, p.B9.

(B) Morales, Gabrielle. "Best Toys for Babies." *Los Alamitos Dispatch*. n. 1, v. 27, Nov. 17, 2003, p.B9.

(C) Morales, Gabrielle. "Best Toys for Babies." *Los Alamitos Dispatch*. v. 27, n. 1, Nov. 17, 2003, pB9.

(D) Morales, Gabrielle. "Best Toys for Babies." *Los Alamitos Dispatch*. v. 27, n. 1, p. B9, Nov. 17, 2003.

The Last LAP

Language Activity Pages

A. Exercising Your Skill

You have been learning about writing an introductory paragraph, supporting paragraphs, and a concluding paragraph for a research report. You have also been learning about writing in-text citations and a bibliography. Number your paper from 1 to 3, and answer the following questions about what you have learned.

1. Which sentence shows how to write an in-text citation correctly?
   (A) Sociology is the study of the social causes and consequences of human behavior (Browning 10).
   (B) Sociology is the study of the social causes and consequences of human behavior—Browning 10.
   (C) Sociology is the study of the social causes and consequences of human behavior. Browning, 10.

2. What is usually the first word listed in each citation in a bibliography?
   (A) author's first name
   (B) title
   (C) author's last name

3. What is the best way to organize an introductory paragraph for a report?
   (A) broad statement that tells the importance of your topic, research statement
   (B) research statement, arguments against your topic
   (C) broad statement that tells the importance of your topic, arguments against your topic, research statement

B. Expanding Your Skill

Number your paper from 1 to 2, and choose the correct way to write a citation for the given type of source.

1. Book
   (A) Nimoy, James. *Spock*. Space Age Press: New York, NY, 1996.
   (B) *Spock*. Nimoy, James. New York, NY: Space Age Press, 1996.
   (C) Nimoy, James. *Spock*. New York, NY: Space Age Press, 1996.
   (D) James Nimoy. *Spock*. New York, NY: Space Age Press, 1996.

2. Encyclopedia
   (B) "Indonesia." *Global Encyclopedia*. 2004 ed.
   (A) *Global Encyclopedia*. 2004 ed. "Indonesia."
   (C) "Indonesia." 2004 ed. *Global Encyclopedia*.
   (D) 2004 ed. *Global Encyclopedia*. "Indonesia."

C. Exploring Language

Expository Writing Read the paragraph below. Choose the best summary for the paragraph.

Alaska is rightly called the "Last Frontier." It is the largest state in the United States, yet it has the smallest population per square mile. Alaska is so big, it has the northernmost, easternmost, and westernmost points in the United States. It also has Mount McKinley, the highest point in North America. Alaska has over 129 million acres of forest and 5,580 miles of coastline. For a true frontier adventure, Alaska is the state to visit.

(A) Alaska has 5,580 miles of coastline, and it has the smallest population per square mile.

(B) Alaska has the northernmost point in the United States and over 129 million acres of forest.

(C) Alaska, the largest state in the United States, has a wide variety of geographical features that are worth visiting, and it has been nicknamed the "Last Frontier."

D. Expressing Yourself

Choose one of these activities. When you are finished, give your paper to your teacher.

1. Complete the following steps for a report about your state.
   a. Choose a topic.
   b. Write a research statement.
   c. Use at least three different sources to research your topic.
   d. Take notes.
   e. Summarize your research. Remember to paraphrase.
   f. Write an outline.
   g. Write an introductory paragraph.
   h. Write three supporting paragraphs.
   i. Write a concluding paragraph.
   j. Write in-text citations.
   k. Write a bibliography.

2. WORK with a PARTNER Find information about your state in ten different sources. Evaluate and compare the different types of information you found. Present your findings to the class.

RESEARCH Scope and Sequence • *Specific Skill Series for Language Arts*

Unit/Level	Level A	Level B	Level C	Level D	Level E	Level F	Level G	Level H
Unit 1	Parts of a Book	Using a Library	Using a Library	Using a Table of Contents	Using a Table of Contents and an Index	Getting Ideas and Narrowing a Topic	Getting Ideas and Narrowing a Topic	Getting Ideas and Narrowing a Topic
Unit 2	Using Books	Using a Table of Contents	Using a Table of Contents	Using an Index	Using an Encyclopedia	Formulating Questions	Formulating Questions	Formulating Questions
Unit 3	Using a Table of Contents	Using an Encyclopedia	Using an Index	Finding Magazine and Newspaper Articles	Finding Magazine and Newspaper Articles	Making a Research Statement	Making a Research Statement	Making a Research Statement
Unit 4	Using a Table of Contents	Key Word Searching	Using an Encyclopedia	Key Word Searching	Key Word Searching	Finding Information	Finding Information	Finding Information
Unit 5	Using an Encyclopedia	Evaluating a Web Site	Key Word Searching	Evaluating a Web Site	Evaluating a Web Site	Using a Table of Contents	Using an Atlas	Using an Atlas
Unit 6	Using an Encyclopedia	Reading a Chart	Evaluating a Web Site	Getting Ideas	Reading Graphs and Charts	Finding Newspaper and Magazine Articles	Finding Newspaper and Magazine Articles	Finding Newspaper and Magazine Articles
Unit 7	Reading a Chart	Taking a Survey	Reading a Chart	Asking Questions	Getting Ideas and Narrowing Your Topic	Key Word Searching	Key Word Searching	Key Word Searching
Unit 8	Taking a Survey	Reading a Diagram	Taking a Survey	Making a Research Statement	Formulating Questions	Evaluating Web Sites	Evaluating Web Sites	Evaluating Web Sites
Unit 9	Finding Information	Getting Ideas	Reading a Diagram	Finding Information	Making a Research Statement	Reading Graphs and Charts	Reading Graphs and Charts	Reading Graphs and Charts
Unit 10	Taking Notes	Asking Questions	Getting Ideas	Comparing Information across Sources	Identifying Sources	Comparing Information across Sources	Comparing Sources	Comparing Sources
Unit 11		Making a Research Statement	Asking Questions	Evaluating Information	Comparing Information across Sources	Taking Notes	Taking Notes	Taking Notes
Unit 12		Finding Information	Making a Research Statement	Taking Notes	Taking Notes	Summarizing	Summarizing	Summarizing
Unit 13		Taking Notes	Finding Information	Summarizing	Summarizing	Writing an Outline	Writing an Outline	Writing an Outline
Unit 14			Evaluating Information	Writing an Outline	Writing an Outline	Writing Introductory Paragraphs	Writing Introductory Paragraphs	Writing Introductory Paragraphs
Unit 15				Writing Paragraphs	Writing Introductory Paragraphs	Writing Supporting Paragraphs	Writing Supporting Paragraphs	Writing Supporting Paragraphs
Unit 16				Writing a Bibliography	Writing Supporting Paragraphs	In-Text Citations	In-Text Citations	In-Text Citations
Unit 17					Writing Concluding Paragraphs	Writing Concluding Paragraphs	Writing Concluding Paragraphs	Writing Concluding Paragraphs
Unit 18					Writing a Bibliography	Writing a Bibliography	Writing a Bibliography	Writing a Bibliography